It's an App World

The Mobile Native's Guide to Marketing

It's an App World

The Mobile Native's Guide to Marketing

Aurelie Guerrieri

App Annie

ISBN-13: 978-0692892961

Library of Congress Catalog Number: 2017908093
Business & Economics / Marketing / General

Published by Akila One

Cover design by Lou Strano

Interior layout by Book Connectors,
www.BookConnectors.com

TABLE OF CONTENTS

PREFACE

More than twenty years ago, I was developing apps for scientific HP calculators. I loved to see that much power concentrated on such a small device, and, I suppose, in my own hands. Some time later, I got my first mobile phone, and then moved to China, where it became clear to me that mobile technology was the way of the future for billions of people around the world.

Mobile is that rarest of technology that's become bigger and more pervasive than expected by most. It has changed the way the world communicates, defined a generation, and set the course for the future of advertising and global commerce.

How I live, work, play, connect, travel, eat, read, and pay is defined by my phone and the apps on it. Every year, phones and apps evolve to deliver even more incredible experiences and in just a few short years we will be able to do even more that will impact our productivity, healthcare, community, safety, entertainment and more. Today these functions are primarily delivered via our smartphones. Tomorrow the smartphone will control apps that are distributed across even more devices—beyond watches and set-top boxes, and interact with our glasses, cars, homes and more. They will become the conduit over which businesses reach, converse and engage with their customers in a way never before thought possible.

It is clear that this medium is maturing and transforming virtually all industries. Smartphones have become a digital appendage, a device on which, we at App Annie have learned, the average user spends more than 2 hours and 15 minutes per day—more than a month out of every year.

Smartphones, and increasingly apps, have become a must-have. For younger generations, it's even more central to how they live, work and play. Mobile's inexorable progress will make us, and every generation that follows, *Mobile Natives* in the truest sense. That's very good news for the marketer as it means that channel innovation is moving up the adoption curve, from experimental pilots to large scale commercialization and profit optimization.

These essential truths demand that mobile know-how becomes a must-have for marketers, bringing as much opportunity as risk. As mobile marketing becomes more of a business driver, the marketer's skill set needs to continue evolving to master ever more complex analytical and technical aspects. Mobile affords unmatched campaign transparency and performance traceability. It's finally the end of the old Madison Avenue saying, "Half the money I spend on advertising is wasted; the trouble is, I don't know which half."

Seven years ago, App Annie set out to take the pulse of the nascent app universe. Today, we use data science and machine learning to measure the rhythms and patterns of consumption and derive a sort of digital encephalogram of a living world and a living earth. During the Gold Rush, you had a guide selling the maps about where to go, where not to go, and that was something very powerful. That's what we're doing with App Annie.

Direct, 24/7, access to consumers through a personal and customizable communication channel is a boon for brands looking to connect and engage their audience. However, understanding and mastering this tool requires a deep knowledge of the underlying technology and tremendous respect and sensitivity for the *Mobile Native*. But what shall we most closely consider?

The amounts of real-time data captured from smartphones and apps is massive. Deriving insights from that data requires analytical skills that used to belong to statisticians rather than marketers. The unfair marketing advantage comes from the ability to map this data to tell us where the *Mobile Native* is going, what they're going to do, and how we can find them in key moments and please them with utility, or entertainment. The marketer, now essential to technology choices as well as revenue generation and customer and client engagement, is not only a support role, but a key decision-maker for the business.

There are three trends shaping mobile marketing today: social communications and, in particular, messaging (not exclusive to Facebook anymore); video (where generation X is the SMS generation, and generation Y the Facebook generation, generation Z favors video as primary communication medium); and programmatic advertising (the marketer becomes a trader on advertising markets that resemble financial markets).

Tomorrow, nascent technologies like geolocation targeting, virtual and augmented reality, new user interfaces, and emergent connected devices will add to the diversification of our marketing channels. These innovations, coupled with evolving consumer behaviors, will offer a plethora of opportunities and challenges to brands.

In this bold future, the mobile marketer will require tremendous expertise to be successful: the soul of an artist, the skills of an analyst, and the resolve of an entrepreneur. It's not just about mobile technology, it's about how marketers chart their own journey to meet mobile users on their own terms. For those marketers who would become master of the mobile medium, nothing—*nothing*—will be more crucial than understanding, and having deep empathy for, the *Mobile Native*.

BERTRAND SCHMITT   *App Annie Co-founder and CEO*

INTRODUCTION

The mobile revolution is almost twenty years old. We have gone from a phone whose only function was to 'transmit voice' (as per its Greek etymology, *télé-phone*) to a smartphone that merges voice and data, jukebox and radio, television and cinema, GPS and payment card into a few square inches.

This device, that fits comfortably in the palm of your hand, is beginning to acquire an intelligence of its own. It is no longer a low level mechanical operating system. It's evolved into an artificial intelligence that recognizes you and anticipates daily activities, both large and small. Our relationship with these devices is transformative and the mobile revolution is still in motion.

Brands have turned to mobile as a new medium to connect with consumers right in the palm of their hands—a much more intimate experience than driving past a billboard and other old-fashioned media.

Historically, print media grew from 1850 on, radio from post-World War I and television from World War II. The world had been waiting for over half a century for a new media and was ripe for being transformed by mobile.

First came voice, then games and content on black and white screens, then finally on color screens. "Applications" started the second mobile revolution, and have given birth to an industry worth billions of dollars: $1 billion, purchase price of Instagram by Facebook, $20 billion, the value of WhatsApp estimated by Facebook.

"Apps" as they are better known, have become widely adopted and are so easily understood by the market that it has allowed the emergence of "pure players;" companies that are exclusively present on mobile, at gigantic valuations. While WhatsApp was valued, at the time of its purchase, at $20 billion, the market cap of a historic mobile operator, T-Mobile, was $27 billion. WhatsApp, in its "application" format, has 450 million users, as many customers as the telecommunications giant Vodafone group.

For many giants of the old economy, the mobile revolution is more like a cataclysm. It's gone beyond being just a new format, and has its own economy and ecosystem. An economy that, according to the analytics firm App Annie, generated $50 billion in 2016, and is projected to reach $110 billion in 2020. It is an ecosystem that few brands master in its entirety. Apple, Google, Microsoft, and Amazon are the big winners of this new mobile era where the brands of the old economy are no more than suppliers or customers or partners at best. This is already true in commerce and telecom but will soon be the case in the automobile, home, health, and financial services.

A crop of mobile first companies are emerging as winners too. They understand mobile phones' unique capabilities and leverage them to the transcend incumbent industries' barriers. Uber is an excellent example of using mobile phones as a platform for direct contact between individuals and by-passing the established moats of taxi companies. That concept is replicable and applicable across many industries.

Finally, the video game industry has also had to reinvent itself. This segment of the market, the most important on the cultural scene, a weapon of massive distraction ahead of television or cinema, experienced two revolutions: first, one of format and then, one of revenue model. Here again, the unit of measurement is in billions of dollars. Tencent, a Chinese Internet giant, acquired SuperCell, the app developer, and publisher of Clash of Clan, for $8.6 billion, while Activision bought King.com, app developer, and publisher of Candy Crush for $5.9 billion. Supercell, a company created in 2010 and whose only product is intangible, is now worth more than the NYSE-listed Hyatt Hotels which owns or operates 680 hotels in the world.

In a certain way, it is now possible to assert that mobile-savviness has become one of the markers predicting the future survival of a company. The digital transformation that brands attempt to undergo in a sort of hyper-accelerated Darwinian mutation passes through mobile as a medium. Therefore, one must wonder about the prospects for those big companies remaining out of the mobile loop...

Mobile marketing is also experiencing a growth crisis as there is a limited number of distribution channels for apps. You can even count them on one hand: the Apple App Store, Google's Google Play, the Microsoft Windows Store and the Amazon App Store. They integrate into an ecosystem-based logic where the hardware (mobile or tablet) supports integrated services and product offerings including operating systems, search engines, browsers, billing or monetization. This oligopoly causes congestion, slowness and critical difficulties of discovery.

Also, the number of applications available on these channels is becoming too large. There are well beyond 2 million apps available on the App Store and the Google Store. How can an application be seen, discovered, and understood in these overcrowded spaces?

Finally, strict rules sometimes constrain the very nature of applications. The four Ps of marketing (Product, Price, Placement, and Promotion) are, to varying degrees, under the tutelage of large manufacturing silos. What kind of new distribution models could make the user experience more fluid, facilitate serendipity, and lay the foundation for a trillion-dollar market? How can we reconcile fluidity and naturalness with a walled-off environment? By an artificial intelligence that will download applications by itself? By Instant Messengers – smart text communication tools that can natively embed or dynamically call these apps from a keyword slipped into the conversation? By the emergence of independent, alternative App Stores (especially in China)? Which of these models will be the source of disruption?

There are still other challenges for mobile marketers. Device fragmentation is one of the most critical challenges. How can one produce content that can adapt to the wide variety of devices on the market, referring to multiple screen sizes, resolutions, operating system versions, and computing power?

Understanding and effecting the consumer journey is another equally important challenge. How does a marketer maintain a continuity of brand experience in a multiplicity of access modes, from paper to a variety of electronic terminals - smart TV, computer, mobile, tablet and now connected objects such as Amazon Echo?

This also raises the question of the compatibility of these manufacturing silos, walled-off universes, sometimes proprietary, sometimes semi-open. How does a marketer build a seamless experience when a user is evolving across such a heterogeneous environment?

The ultimate challenge is the ubiquity of uses. Indeed, beyond the device, the questions of "when" and "where" are also central. Where is the consumer at the time of use? At home, in transportation, at work, in a shop? What are they doing? What frame of mind are they in? Who's with them? Understanding the answers to these question gives brands the ability to deliver a relevant message, conditional upon a multitude of variables representative of a moment.

The mobile ecosystem also includes a "martech" segment, in which technological solutions help capitalize on marketing opportunities during the user experience. The monetization of this traffic, initially started as invasive, then became more creative, and is even now possibly valuable to the user, in the sense that it can sometimes predict attrition and propose re-engagement offers that improve lifetime value. This is one of the strong advantages of mobile marketing products: they enable precise knowledge and targeting of the customer when traditional media can only roughly segment their audience. However, the reality of accuracy is still far from the theory for many of these technologies, as evidenced by "cross-device" tracking.

The large manufacturing silos will be among the winners of this mobile marketing battle. Apple, Google, and Microsoft have been working for years to develop tools, services, and products to identify and support a user in their digital experience. Other newer players emerge, such as Facebook, which knows all about us (what we declare but also what it understands) and can target *ad hominem* messages regardless of the medium: PC, mobile, tablet, and soon in virtual reality.

These American giants often have doppelgangers in China, Russia and sometimes India. Mobile is already strategic to the BRICs' economy and politics today, and will be a source of growth for the next decade. It is imperative for a mobile marketer to understand what is going on there and how to address these specific markets.

This book is meant to provide the keys to understanding this digital revolution. At a time when Fortune 50 companies are pressured by the impetus of a digital transition, their current and future executives will need to know the map to this unfamiliar territory and its immense field of possibilities. This content is also intended for mobile marketers, whose open-mindedness and need to understand this ever quickly changing world, drives them to capitalize on feedback and specific cases.

Drawing from personal expertise as well as contributions from academics, mobile marketers, and innovators, the author deliver a 360-degree approach - theoretical, strategic, and operational - enabling any player in the value chain to deepen their knowledge base and raise their profile as digital marketer.

We'll begin this discussion from a theoretical viewpoint. What are the rules of the game, the universal intangibles to which every end customer responds? What are the models of marketing adoption? What are the clues to understand mobile user engagement? What are the limits of an ever-finer tracking of a customer who also happens to be a citizen governed by an inviolable social and legal pact?

We will then explain the principles of customer acquisition. To exist in the digital space is no longer just to develop an application. What was an end a few years ago now becomes a beginning. To exist is to embody a user experience, a functional and emotional link. In a nutshell: to be used. Thus, a set of players have positioned themselves on the value chain between the mobile needs of a brand and the customer experience, each segment with its own objectives and expectations, sharing a common language: the Key Performance Indicators (KPIs).

The approach will be both strategic, for example with an eco-systemic viewpoint that explains the key strengths and movements of the sector, and completely pragmatic: who are the players in the value chain? How to build a mobile campaign? How to understand engagement and re-engagement? How can one master all distribution channels, App Stores and beyond?

Finally, we'll review the other tenant of mobile marketing: monetization. Lest we forget that media and content are created through and for monetization, the keystone of the entire ecosystem. Without revenues, there is no press, no content, no counter-power. Without revenues, there is no creation, no development, and no applications. That would take us back to a 'digital Stone Age'.

In a rapidly changing technical environment, how do we address these needs and anticipate changes?

We present here the choices and options offered and the tools to understand them and to implement them. We'll arm the reader with a simple but complete approach to understanding budget allocation, launching and optimizing campaigns. We will address the following questions: how to define a strategy; how to understand and choose business models; how to define a tactic; and lastly; how to understand and define media planning, technical options, and constraints.

PART 1

MOBILE BEHAVIORAL CONCEPTS

The consumer has the upper hand with a mobile phone in theirs.

With each new mobile activated, a new consumer profile is born, ever better informed and ever fickler.

The mobile phone is more than an object; it is a tool that allows, even demands, markets to evolve. Fast and accessible, mobile phones have changed the behaviors of consumers, therefore demanding the same of marketers. It used to be that the supply-side controlled the information flow, and therefore somehow the power. But with mobile, this is inverted, and that makes all the difference in the world.

The first part of this book deals with contributions of academic research to mobile marketing. Appearing, in turn, as a tool for brand management, or a revolution in the sense of Kuhn (1962), mobile marketing has meritoriously stirred debate within the scientific community, and simultaneously engendered a fertile, and almost unlimited, operational field.

In this part, the first chapter deals with profiling the mobile phone user—the practice of trying to understand this new individual from an attitudinal and behavioral point of view. The second chapter describes how brands can respond to this new individual by presenting several mobile user's behavioral models and outlining possible strategies for engaging users.

CHAPTER 1
A MOBILE USER PROFILE

Executive summary

· **The profile of the mobile phone user** is complex to comprehend as it is multi-factorial. The quest for immediacy and thirst for experience seem to be the driving forces that motivate and characterize the mobile phone user's navigation and shopping habits.

· **The tie between phone and consumer** seems to have reached a point of no return in modern consumption methods, and even lifestyle. Societal tidal waves, such as the Pokémon Go phenomenon (summer of 2016), continue to prove it.

The main characteristics

Who is the mobile phone user? It is as if this tool, the mobile phone, has become indispensable and even as vital as the air one breathes. This digital omnipresence in our societies reaches such an extent that it can lead some individuals to a real addiction.

DIGITIZED WORLD, DIGITIZED CONSUMER

Some figures are head-turning. In an era of global growth slow down, the results observed in the mobile phone market are staggering. Whether on the consumer or investor side, digital has become a must.

On the supply side, according to eMarketer (2015), the global m-advertising market is expected to reach $100 billion in 2016, which should account for more than 50% of digital advertising spend, and reach 70% by 2019.

On the demand side, in digital marketing generally, but more particularly, in mobile marketing, all indicators show an explosion of investment and consumption. Developed markets show almost saturated smartphone penetration rates (around 70% in the US and Western Europe), while BRICs and other high growth countries are catching up quickly with up to 50% penetration[1]. Over 60% of smartphone users have purchased on mobile in the last 6 months. Criteo expects m-commerce to represent 70% of global e-commerce in 2017— in the US, the share would be over 50%[2]. This is driven by a higher incidence and frequency of m-purchases, but also a higher average basket size. All in all, m-commerce is growing 15 times faster than e-commerce, according to Retail-MeNot[3].

Late 2016 marked a tipping point: more users around the world started accessing the internet from mobile devices (51.2%) than from desktop computers (48.7%)[4]. Consumers around the world became "mobile first".

On average, individuals look at their mobile phones 160 times a day, with 80% of their time spent on apps (games, social networks, news sites applications), according to a Google study in 2015. 84% of mobile phone users surf the Internet almost daily on their mobile phone. App Annie found that users spend more than 2 hours and 15 minutes per day on their mobile phone.

< FOCUS >

MILLENNIALS

Whether they are called "Millennials," "digital natives," "Generation Y" or "WE-I generation," they are individuals who were born between the 1980s and 2000s, that is, at the same time as digital. This hyper-connected population now represents nearly 80 million in the United States and 364 million in China. Millennials make an average of two purchases per week via mobile. Sources: LSA, March 2016; Quantcast (2016), "Mobile + Me".

---

1 Newzoo, Global Mobile Market Report, April 2017
2 OuterBox Design, 2017, US
3 Center for Retail Research & RetailMeNot, eCommerce and mCommerce in Europe and North America, 2016
4 StatCounter

AN ADDICTED CONSUMER

The key to understanding the actions of this new individual is their quest for mobility and movement. Without questioning whether it is technology or human thought that drives the other (*The Edge*, 2010), we must note that the consumer of the 21st century is marked by the seal of mobility and connection.

A hypermodern existence

For Jauréguiberry (2007)[5], in the postmodernist logic, the individual "is free on a free market, the channel-surfing individual builds a life whose programming would have no other object than the satisfaction of immediate desires and expectations. Opportunities and choices multiplying, life becomes like surfing—a quest for thrills and sometimes aesthetic in situations that, like waves, would be both ephemeral and constantly renewed in a sort of perpetual motion."

< FOCUS >

VOYEURISM AT ITS WORST

Live streaming is the epitome of the trend of always closer to real-time, always closer to real-life. Without post-production editing, moderation or content approval, it is as near to a 'raw feed' as one can get. Whether through dedicated apps such as Twitter's Periscope, or within existing apps such as Facebook Live, users can live stream videos taken anywhere in the world, allowing other registered users on the platform to view them, sometimes within a time limit. While those tools weren't developed with nefarious purposes in mind, users have given it a sometimes dubious, even dramatic exploitation. In the quest for instant fame, some users have taped themselves assaulting a special needs classmate (Facebook Live, Chicago, January 2017) or staging their own suicide (Facebook Live, Miami, January 2017). Other fails are less serious but they still pose problems for their authors: when the former French President Francois Hollande decided to use Periscope as a modern social dialog platform, his communication team did not disable live comments and the feed quickly turned into a digital roasting session that contributed to discredit his authority.

5   Jauréguiberry, F. (2007), *Tic et Société*, Vol. 1, p.1-18

The work of Aguilera, Guillot, and Bonin (2009)[6] complements this representation of the interest of using virtual tools, namely that they allow a permanent reorganization of the life of the individual in recalculating the constraints and opportunities emanating from their real lives. In other words, the tool becomes a driver of behavior.

< FOCUS >

FROM SPATIAL MOBILITY TO DEVICE MOBILITY

According to sociologists Viard (2006)[7] and Jauréguiberry (2007), four factors explain this phenomenon:

- · Job market flexibility (post-Fordism): the classical pattern of employment being broken, and the hourly format evolving, employees' commuting modes change in a more fluid way.

- · Feminization of the labor market with a more flexible, less structured organization of women in their daily routines.

- · Forced suburban living of employees in large metropolitan areas, resulting in individuals spending more and more time in transit.

- · The pursuit of increasingly lengthy studies, punctuated by stays in different cities and countries.

These four societal trends mean that the individual wishes to remain active all the time and not to remain "doing nothing" (Jauréguiberry, 2007). When in transit, for example, the individual who suffers from all the time wasted, wishes to use this time for herself. The smartphone becomes a tool for "selfishness". "Mobile phones, as instruments of real-time (immediacy), are used to fight against the reality of time that resists in the form of slowness, lateness, time-outs or delays," (Jauréguiberry, 2007).

---

6 Aguiléra, A., Guillot, C. & Bonin, O. (2009), *Conference Proceedings of the COST*, t.298, p.397-406
7 Viard, J. (2006) *Eloge de la mobilité: essai sur le capital temps libre et la valeur du travail*

As Urry (2005)[8] points out, 'interrelated digital mobility systems are at the very heart of contemporary societies.' The territory that the consumer is investing is no longer simply physical, such as a store, but can also be virtual. "A territory is analyzed not as a fixed and closed container for human actions, but as the product of the encounter, at a particular point in the topographic space, of a set of networks and varied flows that combine into a specific and evolving assemblage." Mobility is therefore well-conceptualized as being multidimensional with the association and imbrication of real and virtual behaviors. As noted by Jauréguiberry (2007), the use of mobile phones has allowed "a return to time ... by a duplication of time thanks to the simultaneous superposition of a media time to a physical time".

< FOCUS >

IS NOMOPHOBIA SERIOUS?

Nomophobia is defined as fear of being without your phone, a combination of the words no, mobile and phobia. In a "hypermodern" logic, that is to say, a quest for unconstrained hedonism (Lipovetsky, G. Charles, S., 2004), the individual develops an addiction, the inability to do without a smartphone. The paroxysm of this addiction is called flow. This mental state leads the individual to lose spatiotemporal markers, too absorbed in fun mode to perform a simple task, such as Internet browsing (Roederer, Filser, 2015).

The insertion of digital in this hypermodernity

An Omnicom Media Group study (2013) shows that an individual uses his smartphone while simultaneously doing something else: in 63% of the cases, he waits for someone or something; in 49%, he uses his smartphone while in transit; in 41% watching TV; 31% listening to music; 26% working; 24% talking; and 15% shopping. In summary, according to Gonzales, Hure, and Picot-Coupey (2012)[9], the smartphone embodies a threefold characteristic - "accessibility" (ease and permanence with which consumers can access the service), "ubiquity" (use your smartphone anywhere), and "all in one" (ability to perform multiple tasks, personal or business, and ability to do it simultaneously).

8   Urry, J. (2005), *Cahiers Internationaux de Sociologie*, 1/2005, p.23-35
9   Gonzales, C. Hure, E, Picot-Coupey, K. (2012), *Usages et valeurs des applications mobiles pour les consommateurs : quelles implications pour les distributeurs?*

< FOCUS >

SMARTPHONE DETOX, THE RIGHT TO DISCONNECT

Therapies are emerging to fight against "infobesity", that is, addiction to electronic media (and not only for professional reasons). These range from common sense approaches (turning off one's mobile as soon as you leave the office), to intensive drug counseling —oh yes; the business of mobile detox is in full swing.

This media time intrudes in all spheres, including private ones. So, Hjorthol and Gripsrud (2009)[10] compared the domestic space not to a haven of peace, but to a "hub" of communication mixing the professional and private spheres.

For Jauréguiberry (2007), "the hunt for lost time, the cult of the rise of urgency, the pressure of the immediate and the multiplication of information plunges the individual into a situation of repeated injunctions to react faster and faster [...]. This acceleration can lead to dizziness, and fall [...]. In a world where everything accelerates and jostles, the connected consumer, placed in a quasi-permanent state of emergency, runs two risks:"

· The traffic jam effect - A congestion of information in too great of a number, forcing the individual to a superficial (thus not satisfactory) treatment.

· Pressure - From a life of emergencies and a sense of not being able to respond.

The two risks are summarized by Jauréguiberry (2007) in his "channel surfer syndrome": "I call "channel surfer syndrome" all the symptoms of the latent evil that threatens those who live too entirely this experience of media ubiquity, to the point of being absorbed. It is at the same time the dissatisfaction of the impossible to find better option, the anxiety of lost time and that of the last minute, the unquenched desire to be here and elsewhere at the same time, the fear of missing something important and not being able to do everything, the stress of hasty choices and the resulting dissatisfaction, the confusion due to ephemeral over-information, the tension between increasing instrumentalization of relationships and a search for deep feelings."

---

10   Hjortol, R., Gripsrud, M. (2009), *Journal of Transport Geography*, p.115-123

ÉRIC BARQUISSAU
Teacher-Researcher at ESC Pau

According to Zenith Optimedia Agency, advertisers will allocate a larger budget in 2017 to mobile ($99.3 billion) than to desktop ($97.4 billion). The mobile advertising market grew by 95% in 2015 and shows impressive momentum globally, led by the Chinese market where 56% of online advertising spending will be on mobile in 2016. But mobile advertising is currently the subject of many debates, at advertisers, advertising agencies or consumers. Of course, there is no question of the relevancy for companies and brands to advertise on mobile, but it is important to note the opportunities, the problems and sometimes even the paradoxes that can be encountered from the behavior of mobile users. For example, consumers sometimes show resistance to advertising strategies, whether on desktop or mobile. In May 2015, PageFair estimated that 200 million people used ad blockers, and that there would be close to 420 million in 2016, a remarkable progression. According to PageFair, 22% of smartphone owners use ad blockers, a percentage still much lower than that of desktop, but growing as ad block-

ers become more ubiquitous on mobile and consumers desire to save on page-loading time, but also not to see advertisements which they consider not to be relevant. In June 2016, the British operator Three even tested offering an ad blocking service, enabling its subscribers to preserve their data plans from ads' consumption. Why such resistance of mobile users vis-à-vis advertisements, whether on mobile web, or in-app? A study by PageFair shows that security concerns and "interruption", a-k-a intrusive ads, are the top two reasons with about 30% each. Seth Godin's permission marketing[11] must become the rule, the alternative bearing the risk of causing increasing discontent.

The lingering paradox is that consumers want to take advantage of free applications, want to browse for free and want to have high value-added information, but do not want to pay for access to these services. However, many sites and applications can finance free content only through advertising,

11   Godin, S. (2007), *Permission Marketing: Turning Strangers into Friends and Friends into Customers*

which is often considered invasive. This, in turn, pressures advertisers and publishers to improve the quality and format of advertising content on mobile (more relevant and less intrusive), optimize weight and duration (and including an option to close the ad), offer truly innovative and personalized ads. This must be balanced against not giving mobile users the impression of being constantly hunted down, and achieved within the context of earning (and keeping) the user's permission to engage. An extremely complex challenge, certainly, but also a very interesting one.

Everything is in place to ensure the sustainable development of the mobile phone. On one side, a hyper-modern consumer provided with a dream tool; on the other, a personalized offer made over a fast, ergonomic medium that creates relational and transactional relationships directly with its target customers. The looming risk that hangs over the market is its potential for extremes, whether in the shape of user addiction, or advertising abuse.

A ubiquitous and experiential being

Mobile's effectiveness goes beyond its original function. Its usage value is reduced to little in the way of its exchange value. In reality, this tool delivers the impossible, that of exercising ubiquity, in a way that still encompasses emotion.

THE GIFT OF UBIQUITY FINALLY GRANTED

With mobile, both the consumer and the advertiser enter into an intense, real and virtual relationship to the extent that one no longer truly knows who is leading the dance.

Physical and virtual space

Mobile phone technology enables the consumer to engage in a truly ubiquitous experience, as Badot and Lemoine (2013) put it. That is, consumers can "acquire goods and services anywhere, anytime and through any physical or electronic interface." As indicated by Salvadore, Menvielle, and Tournois (2013)[12]:

---

12 Salvadore, M., Menvielle, L., Tournois, N. (2013), *Conference on digital marketing research*

"the ubiquity offered by the smartphone made the necessity of a place to connect to the Internet disappear, and has resulted in placing the consumer in an environment that is both physical and virtual. It is now possible for him to move in space while navigating his device, obtain information, or make a purchase. Salvadore (2015)[13], added that "the ubiquity offered by the smartphone contributes to the hybridization of space. This ubiquity allows consumers to interact virtually even when they are physically moving." The paroxysm of this situation of associating physical and virtual space bears a name: phubbing. This neologism (an association of the words "phone" and "snubbing") means that the individual can physically withdraw from a place, or a relationship, by taking refuge in the consultation of their smartphone. This state of affairs is a sign that the consumer today has entered a phase named by sociologists (Lipovetsky and Charles, 2005)[14] and marketers (Cova and Cova, 2006)[15] as "hypermodernity." This is characterized, as Lipovetsky points out, by "the escalation of ever more and ever faster, ever more extreme in all spheres of social and individual life: finance, consumption, communication, information, urban planning, sport, shows. The mobile phone appears as one of the tools, if not the tool of hypermodernity, accessible to all. Indeed, the ergonomics and the practical and polished side (unlike other connected devices such as Google glass, for example) make the smartphone the ideal vector for making an offer, or for creating demand. In both qualitative and quantitative terms, the smartphone appears to be surpassing other virtual tools in a sales environment.

Professionals are unanimous, digital advertising for the sake of digital advertising is unlikely to generate impressive results. Digital marketing must focus on simplifying information sharing and improving the purchasing experience. This objective means that implementing a digital strategy must be accompanied by a change management plan that will impact most functions and most teams in a company.

---

13 Salvadore, M. (2015), *Doctorate Thesis*
14 Lipovetsky, G., Charles, S. (2005), *Hypermodern times*
15 Cova, V., Cova, B. (2006) in Aubert, N. (2006), *The hypermodern individual*

An ally, but of whom?

Digital experiences via the mobile phone can be a killer of brick and mortar stores, but also an ally. Schwab (2016) confirms this by stating that "mobile phones are mainly used to inquire about products, compare prices and look for promotional offers [...] the mobile phone is no longer identified only as a trans-actional device, but as a tool that can redirect consumers to physical outlets. It is a major influencer in the purchasing process."[16] Digital can even be a tool driving traffic to the point of sale. The notions of "mobile to store" or "digital to store" are well-documented. More generally, for Cabezon[17], "the idea is not to return the store customer to the Internet, but to complete (within the store) the offer presented or available online". This author offers stores the following 10 tips to counter showrooming:

- Offer customers a chance to get off their smartphone as a pretext for a "mobile detox" moment;
- Align store pricing with Internet pricing (called "dynamic pricing") and advertise it at the point of sale;
- Be transparent and explain why store prices are higher (for example because these products support local business);
- Communicate on the benefits of in-store purchase (immediacy, product testing);
- Offer store exclusives;
- Give emotion and personalization to each client;
- Use mobile payments to limit lines and shopping cart abandonment;
- Offer participation in an exclusive contest at your point of sale;
- Give a service exclusively to your customers who buy in stores: the right to participate in a tasting workshop, for example; and
- Play the human card: it is essential to develop a trusting, caring relationship for each client.

While some of these suggestions may appear outlandish or reactionary, like the first one, particularly in a world where connected stores represent a vision of the future of retail, it is true that retailers are thinking hard about ways to regain control of the customer relationship. Amid the storm mobile has created, some hope that mobile will also provide solutions.

---

16   Centre for Retail Research & RetailMeNot (March 2016), *eCommerce and mCommerce in Europe and North America*
17   Cabezon, S. (2015), *Internet Marketing, 2014-2015*

For example, Stroz (2015)[18] points out the opportunity to use data to improve in-store customer experience and merchandising effectiveness by "nurturing the desire to buy, by influencing the decision factors until the act of purchase." Here one can see advantages for both the consumer and the supplier, in that the mobile phone redistributes the power between these two parties. But it is certainly not the VRM (Vendor Relationship Management) that will help the brands regains this power unless the VRM is itself driven by the brand.

< FOCUS >

VRM HOW TO

The Vendor Relationship Management (VRM) principle dictates the necessity of providing consumers with a set of tools to manage the relationship between the vendor and themselves (Willart, 2013). It is a matter of rebalancing the relationship, which was in the CRM (Customer Relationship Management) logic to the exclusive advantage of the offer. With the VRM, the consumer controls the data he has shared. VRM appears as a reaction to user tracking and 'big data'. Concretely, some computer tools, such as Privowny, allow for the identification and disabling of cookies. With VRM then, consumers have the means to take control of their relationship with brands.

18   Stroz J. (2015). *Research Thesis*

Indeed, VRM, conceptualized by Harvard University and Searls (2012)[19], provides consumers with the tools to find the products and services best suited to their expectations, based on suppliers' offers. With VRM, the consumer can thus completely free himself from the first service offered by the supplier, namely information, and advice. The consumer manages his relationship with the brands as he sees fit. With this type of tool, the mobile user becomes reinforced in his behavior of free rider: the free rider researches products at retailers that provide a high level of service and information, but purchases them at retailers that provide low prices and little service. The multitude of digital and mobile offers that promise a lower cost, whether they are coupon specialists (Groupon, RetailMeNot, etc.), local directories (Yelp, OpenTable, etc.), or price comparison engines (Decide for example) does not help the retailers keep their hold on the consumer - the consumer takes control of what they want, when they want it and how they want it. This decides Barnes and Scornavacca (2004)[20] to categorize mobile as a media in its own right, much the same as TV, or newspapers.

< FOCUS >

THE PLACES OF INFLUENCE OF THE SMARTPHONE

The ubiquity of using the smartphone is proven, as are the most common places it is used to discover offers and complete purchases:

· At a coffee shop (52%)
· At work (49%)
· In transit (45%)
· In stores (44%)

Source: Tradedoubler study, 2014.

---

19   Searls, D. (2012), *The Intention Economy: When Customers Take Charge*
20   Barnes, S.J., Scornavacca E. (2004), *International Journal of Mobile Communication*, p. 128-139

Mobile's ubiquity offers very tactical benefits: for example, saving time. But, in a hypermodern world, the consumer wants, in addition to the practicalities of discovery and transactions, to be seduced emotionally.

THE REVENGE OF AFFECT AND RE-ENCHANTMENT: MOBILE AS EXPERIENTIAL

Mobile marketing appears as a factor enabling the consumer to live through a real consumer experience, which academic literature has termed experiential marketing. But in the logic of always delivering more, the mobile phone has become the icon of revisited experiences.

A world of emotions

Experimental marketing had been conceptualized by Holbrook and Hirschman (1982)[21] as a weapon of differentiation. In making the customer live an experience that no other had made him live, the brand would generate positive sentiment and gain a competitive advantage. Tired of an environment that "only" offered the real world, the consumer is looking for something else, that even goes beyond the very object he buys and consumes. This other thing is in the realm of magic and irrationality. Beyond the product or the place of purchase, the consumer demands more imagination. According to Caru and Cova (2006), "in the experiential perspective, on the contrary, the consumer seeks less to maximize a profit, than to claim hedonistic gratification in a social context; the consumption provoking sensations and emotions which, far from responding only to needs, go so far as to influence the consumer's quest for identity." In its paroxysm, experiential marketing brings the individual into a state of "flow." This state was defined by Csikszentmihalyi (1997)[22] as an exceptional moment during which "What we feel, what we wish and what we think are in total harmony." All this is well and good except that with the advent of "all mobile," experiential has become the routine state of the mobile user. Through the mobile phone, the individual lives, in essence, the extraordinary, every day, therefore one must go beyond the experiential in a sort of "meta-experiential."

---

21 Holbrook M.B., Hirschman E.C. (1982), *Journal of Consumer Research*, vol. 9, n° 2, p. 132-140.
22 Csikszentmihalyi M. (1997) *Finding Flow*

HEATHROW AIRPORT

Heathrow is the scene of many hit movies (*The Bourne Ultimatum*, *Love Actually*, etc.). The West London airport's name is as identifiable as the world's biggest brands – you can just say 'Heathrow' and people will understand what you're talking about without any need to further define a function or product. However, though Heathrow was frequented by more than 75 million passengers in 2015, it does not own its customer base - they are essentially "borrowed" from the 80 airlines that Heathrow serves.

But that specificity doesn't prevent Heathrow, which boasts more than 70 stores and 40 restaurants, from having a brand strategy. Its marketing pitch? Experience. Heathrow promises to "Make every trip better." This slogan is all the more audacious as experience has not always been its strong point, admits Simon Chatfield, an e-business and CRM manager for Heathrow. To realize its ambition, Heathrow has invested, in recent years, nearly 11 billion pounds in a vast optimization project. "We built a cathedral for travelers," said Simon Chatfield. This choice of words is no ode to tradition - the "Heathrow Cathedral" is resolutely technophile and features many digital interactions.

Via its website and mobile app, the airport offers a galaxy of services, ranging from booking parking spaces and lounge areas, to click-and-collect for duty-free products on sale in its shops. In spearheading the digital airport strategy, Terminals 2 and 5 have been packed with digital kiosks and interactive billboards. "Beacons are currently one of our priorities," adds Chatfield, the objective of these beacons being to increase opportunities for transit customers to login online, thereby feeding the CRM of the airport. The airport is also supported by a free Wi-Fi offering that allows Heathrow to push visitors 50,000 emails a day. "If we know who our customers are, we can define their needs," says Simon Chatfield.

To this end, Heathrow develops user personas, each associated with a typical client journey. Ultimately, it's about the airport defining all the needs of its passengers and developing the appropriate services.

Source: emarketing.fr, May 2016.

Experiential Revisited

Digital tools and the growing power of consumers are poised to revolutionize marketing. This revolution, according to Roederer and Filser (2015)[23], will be marked by a new generation of consumers who are both "mobile and co-producers of their experience." Paradoxically, with the advent of technology, especially in the field of mobile phones, the consumer wants to give and receive emotion. Adami (2013)[24] showed the emotional impact of advertisements on mobile phones by measuring emotional intensity using EEG (electroencephalogram) and eye-tracking (eye movements). Emotion is no longer the enemy of reason, and modern research demonstrates that the two are intertwined. The consumer seeks hedonism and is "in search of sensory and emotional stimuli" (Roederer, Filser, 2015), which experiential marketing precisely offers. While experiential marketing has been defined academically since 1982, it is evolving. The consumer is no longer satisfied with a mere theatricalization of the offer, rather, he wishes to go beyond this stage, in search of a perfect, efficient and fun situation.

Efficiency is one of the keys to the experience. Isaac and Volle (2014) highlight that user satisfaction with navigation influences buying behavior and loyalty for a site. They emphasize that satisfaction must not be limited to functional factors, such as feature richness, responsiveness, and the degree of personalization. It is necessary to add hedonic qualities, such as the aesthetics, novelty and surprise. This is what a study by Activis/Bva Limelight (2016) reveals: for the marketing managers of the 100 largest companies, best practices should focus on four parameters: ergonomics, design, and format but also pleasing content based on video and interaction.

EXAMPLE

VICTORIA'S SECRET

To significantly reduce shopping cart abandonment on its mobile site, Victoria's Secret improved ergonomics. They created a button dedicated to promotions instead of having to enter a promotional code upon checkout.

Source: LSA, March 2015.

---

23 Roederer, C., Filser, M. (2015), *Experiential marketing, towards a co-creative marketing*
24 Adami, M. (2013), *International Journal of Mobile Marketing, Vol 8*, p. 95-103

CLAIRE ROEDERER

Lecturer, University of Strasbourg, author of several books including Experiential Marketing

THE MOBILE USER AND THE EXPERIENTIAL QUEST

Since the 1990s, the use of mobile phones has become widespread. Technological advances have enabled miniaturization, the addition of cameras, touch screens and geolocation. These breakthroughs in mobile phone technology change usage and consumption. The mobile user becomes a more and more common figure. Brands are rethinking their strategies to reflect the brand's experience in various channels, including mobile devices that enable communication and/ or sales by targeting the consumer in real time.

According to recent studies, consumers use their smartphone to call for advice, to take a product picture, and finally to compare prices. Moreover, the mobile is often the last touchpoint before the purchase. These new practices impact the traditional stages of purchasing behavior and the whole experiential process (before experience, buying experience, consumer experience, after experience). Geolocation tools send push alerts (promotions, information, games) to customers' mobile phones when they arrive at the point of sale. The deployment of new technologies (smartphones and social networks) and in-store technical solutions erase the boundary between physical and virtual channels to the benefit of the omnichannel, which intends to deliver a seamless experience, whatever channel is used.

How do brands recognized for their experiential strategies adapt to mobile users? The example of Starbucks is rich with lessons. Indeed, in line with the experiential approach developed by Pine and Gilmore (1999), or Schmitt (1999), the brand has built its success by delivering the very hedonic experience of a European coffee shop, revisited for America. The brand does not sell coffee or even a coffee brand, but the holistic Starbucks experience. In 2015, thanks to improvements to its mobile application, Starbucks crossed a new threshold. Indeed, more than 20% of its transactions in the United States are processed by its mobile app. This unprecedented result places mobile marketing at the heart of the brand's strategic activities. Starbucks' first mobile app dates to 2011. At the time, the company used a QR code-based application as a loyalty card to reward (using free drinks) customers who used the app. In recent years, the application has been redesigned to become a full-fledged experience, allowing consumers to control and pay. The brand also sends promotional messages by the application. The success of the Starbucks application demonstrates how "in-app" messages can increase overall business sales, when, like Starbucks, there is a strong brand image, but above all, a usage in contexts that the company does not control entirely, but in which it can differentiate itself from the competition.

The essentials

· **The world has become digitalized**. Worldwide figures show an exponential growth of the sale of smartphones and of user's connectivity. This generates new behaviors that experiential marketing can capitalize on.

· The smartphone has for some individuals, become so important in their lives, that they have become addicted. More broadly, the profile of a mobile phone user reveals a being in search of immediacy, ubiquity, and simplicity - in short, a **hypermodern being**.

CHAPTER 2

MOBILE USER PURCHASING BEHAVIOR AND APPROPRIATE MARKETING STRATEGIES

Executive summary

· **The intrusion** of smartphones into the daily life of consumers is leading to many changes in the relationship between brands and consumers. The swiftness offered by mobile technology calls for a "situational" vision of marketing which takes into account the contextual variables at purchase time.

· **The result** of this vision is that smartphone usage allows more fluid exchanges between consumers and marketer, and creates real opportunities to develop and boost sales.

Mobile user behavioral patterns

Mobile marketing reshuffles the academic rulebook. Certain marketing concepts become key in understanding the behavior of mobile users. Mobile users can be referred to as "connected shoppers," having developed a *de facto* expertise.

THE IMPORTANCE OF SITUATIONAL MARKETING

In the understanding of consumer behavior, cell phones refocus attention on situational factors. Such factors consider the contextual information to which the consumer is adapting at any given ("T") moment. Thus, "location-based mobile advertising eliminates geographic and informational barriers between consumers and company offers, by reaching consumers when they are within proximity of a merchant location."[1] In effect, cell phones enable us to know the temporal and physical spaces in which the consumer finds himself.

< FOCUS >

THE MOBILE CITIZEN

As of January 1, 2017, cell phones in India have become an anti-aggression tool. All smartphones are equipped with a key called the "panic button." Upon pressing this key, the individual will be geolocated, and help will come to them.

The impact of this immediacy on consumer perception and actions has not always been considered or adequately measured in early marketing models attempting to explain the target's behavior. Personal factors such as socio-demographic and psychological variables were put first.

Eventually, the contextual dimension emerged with the publication of works by Belk (1974, 1975)[2]. To explain the consumer's behavior, he placed contextual data at the center of considerations. He lists five dimensions:

- **Physical** context: composed of polysensory variables such as light, odor, temperature, music and space.
- **Social** context: refers to whether the consumer is alone or accompanied at the point of sale.
- **Temporal** context: refers to factors affecting the moment of purchase such as the season, the day in the month or the time of the day.
- Context of the **role** being played: refers to the psychological role of the individual at the time of purchase. Is he purchasing a product for his own consumption? Is he purchasing a product as a gift?
- Context related to the consumer's **mood** and/or health.

---

1 Rodriguez Goncalves, L., Pechpeyrou, P., Benavent, C., *Revue française du marketing*, Issue 248, p. 27-42
2 Belk, R.W. (1974), *Journal of Consumer Research*, vol. 11, p. 156-163; Belk, R.W. (1975), *Advances in Consumer Research*, vol. 2, p. 427-437

GÉRARD DANAGUEZIAN
CEO of Moby Survey

DISTINCTIVE ADVANTAGES OF MOBILE SURVEYS

The popularity of mobile devices and the specific benefits they offer for the instantaneous collection of "enriched" data make it possible to develop many applications in the field of marketing research. Today's marketer doesn't wonder whether building a mobile survey is appropriate; rather, how to build it and effectively implement CAMI (Computer Assisted Mobile Interviews). This includes choosing between administering the mobile survey via a specific application or via a mobile web browser. Let's focus on the first option.

ADMINISTRATION VIA MOBILE APPLICATIONS

A mobile survey application must first be installed on the user's smartphone or tablet. As a result, they are most often used in the context of a network of researchers, internal auditors or panelists. They are used much less frequently for one-off consumer requests.

The principle advantage of a mobile application is the ability to ensure that research can be conducted offline. This can be useful in areas with weak coverage, and it also saves money when a network of researchers is equipped with tablets without SIM cards (and thus, without an associated data plan). The researchers can carry out their surveys or censuses offline, then upload the information via Wi-Fi once they have returned home or to the company.

A mobile survey application can integrate the following aspects more easily than a web questionnaire:

· Optimized interfaces with ergonomics to facilitate the administration of complex surveys (dynamic filtering, conditional displays, question or answer rotation, non-linear paths, etc.);
· Standardized displays that do not depend on the hardware and web browser used;
· Local storage of data from surveys and associated databases (customer data, historical data, etc.);
· Optimal access to all the mobile device's hardware resources: GPS

coordinates from the location the survey was taken, taking pictures (of merchandising set up, of a product, of a non-conformity, etc.), the ability to read a barcode or a QR code, audio or video recording, etc.;

- New possibilities for interaction with interviewees through simplified presentation of videos, photos or files (PDF...) pre-stored on the device;

- Maximum ease and speed of deployment both to the researchers' locations and for the retrieval of collected responses; and

- Improved data security since the data is stored on the mobile device before being transferred to the server (with the possibility of preserving a backup even after synchronization).

Before the mobile age, the marketer knew that these five factors were very important to know and manipulate, but she was not able to accurately leverage them. With mobile marketing, it is now completely conceivable. Geolocation makes it possible to better define the immediate environment of the consumer. As a first step, brands can collect data on their target customers. The physical context (e.g. the city and street in which the individual is located), the social context (e.g. the interaction with other internet users) and the temporal context are immediately identifiable, with certainty. By cross referencing this information with other data, the context of the role being played and the context of mood can be deduced. Consequently, brands can create personalized offers that are better adapted to the context experienced or felt by the target.

< FOCUS >

AN OBJECTIVE CONTEXT TO BE DISTINGUISHED FROM A SUBJECTIVE CONTEXT

Mobile devices take the context into account in an objective way, and unfortunately, run into the problem of evaluating the context as it is experienced psychologically by the consumer.

While Belk has made considerable progress in marketing research, his work is nonetheless open to criticism in the sense that the consumer's perception of the situation has not been taken into account. Thus, Wicker (1975)[3], as well as Lutz and Kakkar (1975)[4] have highlighted the fact that an "objective" context must be distinguished from a "subjective" context. The latter appears to them to be a determining factor in the assessment of consumer behavior.

Therefore, the brand's adaptation to the client's context becomes paramount. For example, it would be counterproductive in terms of persuasion to send messages via mobile devices that are out of sync with the context that the target is experiencing. The individual develops a positive attitude and behavior toward messages that he sees as useful in relation to his context, as confirmed in an empirical study by Khelladi, Castellano and Limongi (2014)[5]: "it is not enough to personalize the advertising message based on the consumer's profile. The message must be conveyed at the most appropriate time." For example, with respect to emails, a study by Experian Cheetahmail (2010) indicates that "the opening rate is higher on Mondays (18.2%), Fridays (17.9%) and Thursdays (17.8%). In terms of time slots, the end of the day (6:00 PM to 9:00 PM) is the most appropriate timeframe to elicit a response. For text messaging, the most appropriate time slots would be during the day as individuals keep their mobile devices close by."[6] This clearly shows the psychological power of the environment on the behavior of the individual. This is similar to the work of Barsalou (1983)[7] on the classification of objects (called categorization) in the

---

3   Wicker, A.W. (1975), *Journal of Consumer Research*, vol. 2, p. 165-167
4   Lutz, R.J., Kakkar, P. (1975), *Advances in Consumer Research*, Vol. 2., p. 439-454
5   Khelladi, I., Castellano, S., Limongi, L. (2014), *Revue française du Marketing*, p. 43-58
6   Dianoux C. et al (2012), *Management & Avenir*, 2012/8, p.189-208
7   Barsalou, L. (1983), *Memory & Cognition* 11 (3), p. 211-227

individual's environment based on their usefulness. Indeed, the individual hierarchizes the relevance of the information he receives, and therefore, in the context of mobile marketing, the relevance of the advertising messages he receives, according to his personal objectives. The major difficulty for the mobile marketer is identifying the individual's motives, not purely based on location, but based on the target's pursued goals. As a result, localization is not always the best indicator of motivation. For example, an individual might be close to a cinema, but this does not mean that he is going to see a movie.

< FOCUS >

FROM DIGITAL TO PHYGITAL

Karine Motch of Extreme Sensio explains that "the interest of phygital is to bring the best of digital into the context of the physical." It is the concept behind the word which is interesting. "Phygital" merges the "physical" and the "digital": it increases the number of bridges between the two channels until the consumer does not differentiate between them. This focus on the consumer ensures that she is given a fluid, seamless experience which will ultimately lead her back to the store. Therefore, the idea is to give the consumer a buying experience that surfs between the sensations linked to her presence at the point of sale and her digital navigation at this same point. The winning recipe requires minimal digital interaction. As Romain Thibault of Unibail Rodamco emphasizes, "digital has to provide the right service at the right time." If digital adds to the decision-making process by complicating one of the steps, there is no point in making the investment to digitize the point of sale.

Source: *LSA*. February 2016.

ACADEMIC MODELS

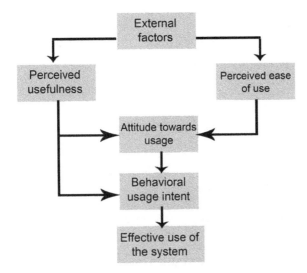

Figure 2.1 – The TAM model

New patterns of mobile consumer behavior are emerging. Dickinger et al. (2004)[8], as well as Scornavacca and McKenzie (2007)[9] have thus integrated mobile-specific variables, such as the timing of messaging or the ergonomics of the device used. These two elements have been shown to be variables which influence the effectiveness of text message campaigns. Others, such as Kavassalis et al. (2003)[10], as well as Bauer et al. (2005)[11] have validated the influence of perceived benefit and perceived risk, respectively. More generally, most researchers agree to take the TAM (*Technology Acceptance Model*) by Davis et al. (1989)[12] as a baseline and to adapt it.

Within the framework of mobile marketing, this model has the advantage of integrating two dimensions specific to the mobile device and its user: the perceived usefulness and the perceived ease of use. Because these two factors determine the attitude of a consumer toward a given technology, they determine the intent to use; however, only the perceived usefulness has a direct impact on the intent to use.

8 Dickinger, A., et al (2004), *An Investigation and Conceptual Model of SMS Marketing*
9 Scornavacca, E., McKenzie, J. (2007), *International Journal of Mobile Communications*, Vol. 5, p. 445-456
10 Kavassalis, P., et al (2003), *International Journal of Electronic Commerce*, Vol. 8, p. 55-79
11 Bauer, H.H. et al (2005), *Journal of Electronic Commerce Research*, Vol. 6
12 This model was completed by the TAM 2 model of Venkatesh and Davis (2000), the UTAUT model of Venkatesh et al (2003) and finally by the TAM 3 model of Venkatesh and Bala (2008)

As mobile advertising is intrusive in nature (discussed later), and as, at the same time, ergonomics has clearly improved, the "perceived utility" variable may, in some cases, become a very important element or even a determining factor in consumer behavior. Therefore, Bruner II and Kumar (2005) proposed the c-TAM (*Consumer Technology Acceptance Model*)[13] which highlights the customer acceptance.

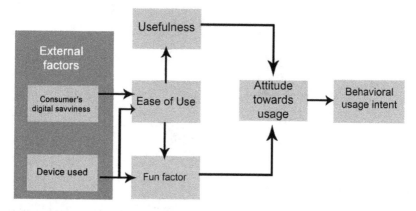

Figure 2.2 – The c-TAM model of Bruner II and Kumar

This model was then completed by Venkatesh *et al.* (2003), who highlighted three types of variables affecting the intent to use:

• Direct determinants of intention: expected performance, expected effort and social influence.
• Direct determinants of use: facilitating conditions and intention to engage in a given behavior.
• Moderating variables: gender, age, experience and context of use.

Venkatesh *et al.* (2003)[14] suggest that other variables can be included: cost of perceived risk, innovation trend and perceived security. In the context of the adoption of mobile services (namely applications), several studies have measured the parameters that motivate purchases. They concluded that the utilitarian value of apps explains their download or purchase, while the hedonic dimension explains the intent to continue using them.

Nevertheless, this model shows different results between application categories, as well as between different cultures. The category variations hold true for m-commerce as well: for example, clothing is more popular with consumers

---

13 Bruner II, C., Kumar, A. (2005), *Journal of Business Research*, 58, p. 553-558
14 Venkatesh, V. et al (2003), *MIS Quarterly*, 27, 3, p. 425-478

living in remote areas than urban customers, who tend to purchase more cultural goods[15]. Furthermore, a 2010 study by the EIAA (European Interactive Advertising Association)[16] demonstrated that when purchasing an airline ticket, 71% of internet users searched for information prior to buying online, while only 8% of users researched when the purchase pertained to food. The different profiles present in the literature imply that segmentation is prevalent in digital behavior. Thus professionals must adapt to these differences; navigation and offers should be tailored precisely to the aforementioned behaviors.

Country	Kenya	Hong Kong	United States of America	Germany	United Kingdom	France
% of total internet consumption via mobile	97%	40%	31%	28%	25%	24%

Table 2.1 – Internet consumption via a mobile device. Comparison between different countries.

SUMMARY

Mobile marketing mobilizes numerous marketing disciplines. We have already stated this, simply because it represents a genuine revolution. With this revolution, a concept stemming from the works of Belk in 1974 emerges (or reappears), as well as adapted adoption models.

Concretely, mobile marketing requires that we consider the consumer's purchasing context. More than ever, the consumer's decision-making process is impacted directly by considering situational data such as place and time. The

marketer must be aware of the importance of these elements by integrating them into his action plan and into his advertising messages. For example, the consumer will be more sensitive, and therefore more reactive to an offer adapted to the place and time of its receipt. The subjective context must be finely analyzed to avoid being counterproductive in terms of persuasion.

---

15 Hjorthol, R. (2009). *Environment and planning. B, Planning & design*, 36, 2, p. 229-26
16 EIAA (2010). *European Mobile Internet Use*

Mandatory Strategy Changes for Brands

In the face of this new mobile user, brands must evolve and consider anew their offers from a 360-degree view. Mobile marketing also offers growth opportunities for brands, but they must be careful not to appear intrusive. This would be counterproductive because "mobile first" rhymes with "user first." This means that the mobile marketer must be vigilant and avoid damaging consumer relationships, especially in terms of privacy. While mobile devices are slowly becoming an indispensable media due to their frequency of use (mobile first), we should not forget that the customer remains the most important priority (user first).

THE REIGN OF CROSS-CHANNEL MARKETING, A 360-DEGREE CONSUMER

The consumer always has his smartphone in his pocket, so the temptation to use it is great. In fact, mobile devices push consumers to adopt omnichannel behaviors. To quote Belvaux and Notebaert (2015)[17]: "he naturally goes from one channel to another, without thinking. Within the same brand, he expects the same services, the same prices and to be recognized, whether he takes a physical or digital path." Many researchers have studied this phenomenon, which upsets the classical view of consumer behavior. Belvaux and Notebaert (2015) state that digital enables the consumer to simplify and streamline the steps in their decision-making process. Recall that there are typically five stages in the process of consumption behavior. Digital makes it possible to reduce the various compromises that are inherent in the purchase of a product or service. Firstly, digital mitigates the lack of information supplied. The consumer is better informed: sometimes even better than the salesperson. Secondly, digital gives the consumer a better understanding of the market in terms of price. Lastly, it allows the consumer to save time.

Hence, there have been several developments since the first management theory models. For example, the sequencing of the various stages followed by the consumer in the purchasing process is no longer as linear. The advent of mobile digital reorganizes the five steps proposed by classic marketing models (identification of need, information retrieval, evaluation of the possibilities offered by the market, purchase and post-purchase evaluation). All of this comes with a very strong personal dimension, for "there are very few objects whose personal characteristic is as marked as that of a mobile phone [...] due to the variety and the sensitivity of the information that they store."[18]

17　Belvaux, B., Notebaert, J.-F. (2015), *Cross-channel and Omnichannel, Digitalization of Customer Relationship*

18　Bourliateux-Lajoinie, S., Stenger, T. (2011), *e-marketing & e-commerce*

This restructuring seems to involve a disturbance within these different phases or even a reduction of the sequencing. With regards to disturbances, Vanheems (2010)[19] shows that the virtual (that is, the mobile phone) reduces the time spent in the real (that is, the physical store) at the time of choice and purchase. As for the sequencing reduction, Kaufman-Scarborough and Linquist (2002)[20] propose two steps rather than five in the buying process as part of cross-channel behavior: preparation and purchase. For their part, Chaffey et al. (2014) state that in the fifth stage dedicated to the post-purchase evaluation, it is necessary to "add a specific dimension of social sharing/recommendation." [21]

---

19 Vanheems, R. (2010), *Colloque 9e journées normandes de recherches sur la consommation*
20 Kaufman-Scarborough, C., Linquist, J.D. (2002), *The Journal of Consumer Marketing, Vol. 19*, p. 333-350
21 Chaffey, D. et al (2014), *Digital Marketing*

SÉBASTIEN MÉGRAUD
Associate director at Mediacrossing,
digital communication agency

Over the last few years, the advertising market has undergone an unprecedented change, with a shift in spending from offline media (display, radio, printed press, etc.) to online/connected media. Today, digital media represents the second largest medium and it is constantly growing. It is proclaimed to be the main medium of the future.

As the main engine of digital growth, mobile media is evolving rapidly, thanks to a high rate of smartphone sales. Now the primary device used to access the internet, smartphones far exceed computers in both number of units sold and in volume of searches on Google[22]. For a successful digital communication strategy, it is now not only necessary to include mobile devices in the media mix, but to build strategy around the mobile device (i.e. apply the "mobile first" concept). In the vein of inbound marketing and permission-based marketing, mobile marketing must bring added value to the user. The user is looking for a service rather than advertising and content rather than design. Success-ful campaigns rely on relevance, convenience, customization and a one-to-one relationship between user and brand. Cornerstone of mobile marketing, user experience (UX) will be a major challenge in the years to come. It sits at the crossroads of consumer needs and brand objectives, and is comprised of three main pillars: context, content and user.

Practically, user experience is influenced by a large number of factors: accessibility, ergonomics, information architecture, user interface, etc. Unlike desktop, it is important to take into account the difference in screen sizes (large fragmentation between 3.5 and 8 inches), the connection speed and the hardware aspects (e.g. gyroscope). The "progressive enhancement" concept incorporates these constraints by providing simple functionality to ensure basic service to all users, regardless of their mobile device, while progressively improving upon the experience, depending on the available equipment.

Beyond websites and mobile applications, the user experience also extends to advertising with the need to offer contextual advertising (e.g. sponsored links in search engines or native ads similar to advertorials) or to stand out through originality. Thus, some banner type campaigns (display) integrate interactivity via rich animations (e.g. a 360-degree video) while others rely mainly on applications and mobile first services (e.g. Snapchat).

The ultimate goal remains conversion; that is, the transformation of a mobile user into a qualified contact or a paying customer. To do this, it is essential to create call-to-action buttons and to define a conversion funnel. Despite having reached technological maturity, mobile devices remain, for the moment, a media that is largely underexploited by advertising, which opens up many exciting prospects.

The place of mobile devices (and more broadly, of the virtual world) in these two phases has been envisioned in two ways. Some studies have shown that the virtual world has a preponderant place in the first sequence (the click-and-mortar model, or, as it's called in one of its iterations, ROPO, Research Online, Purchase Offline). A DigitasLBI (2015) study also shows that 68% of smartphone owners say that they are ready to receive personalized and geo-targeted discounts or promotions on their mobile phones. This fact leads Cabezon (2015) to state that "the mobile device becomes a tool to *drive to shop*." Others (Belvaux, 2006[23]; Schröder and Zaharia, 2008[24]) have shown the opposite; that is, the virtual world is used more as a place to order products following a physical visit to a point of sale (the mortar-and-click model, also called showrooming). A study by Google (2015)[25] also shows that 24% of consumers use their smartphone in-store to compare prices. This research, which can be described as binary, may be too restrictive in its attempt to give a "before-and-after" chronology. Badot et Lemoine (2013)[26] have shown that the digital and physical worlds are intertwined at each stage in a sort of constant back-and-forth. This navigation between the virtual and the real creates an "e-shopping experience." Roederer and Filser (2015) indicate that "whereas multichannel refers to a compartmentalized view between the physical store and the online store, omnichannel assumes that customers move freely between online tools, mobile devices and the physical store, all within the purchase cycle of the same transaction." It is up to the brands to respond to this new behavior through real-time marketing.

23 Belveaux, B. (2006), *Revue française de marketing*, p.49-68
24 Schröder, H., Zaharia, S. (2008), *Journal of Retailing and Consumer Services*, Vol. 15, p. 452-468
25 Google (2015), *Moments that Matter Research*
26 Badot, O., Lemoine, J.F. (2013), *Recherches et Applications en Marketing*, Vol. 28, p. 3-13

Thus, Badot and Lemoine (2013) evoke the different shapes that this "e-shopping experience" can take, including the "brick and tap" (store + smartphones): in one case, the consumer is encouraged to perform online searches while in the store, or to download m-coupons for the products he has in front of him; in another case, "around me" features help the consumer locate retail stores nearby, according to his geolocation.

OPPORTUNITIES FOR BRANDS

With mobile technology, targeting is not just an empty word. Smartphones are personal items, rarely lent to others. As a result, they enable nearly certain identification of the owner. Thus, the message addressed to her can be personalized like never before in the history of advertising. It is, in some ways, the culmination of "one to one," for it associates the contextualization with the consumer. Geofencing is an example of application. It consists in defining virtual borders and detecting consumers as soon as they enter an area, and triggering relevant messages (coupons, promotions). These Location Based Services (LBS) are personalized offers (coupons, promotions) that take into account the geographical area. As Isaac and Volle (2013) point out, "while traditional marketing relies on the memorization of background information conveyed by advertising media, the availability of information - directly useful in decision making, at the place and time of purchase – is going to revolutionize communication strategies. Will we spend millions of dollars to make the masses of consumers memorize messages which will (possibly) be useful to them in a day, a week or a month... or to deliver the right information to the individual at the right moment via their mobile phones?"

Digital media presents opportunities for the development of new offerings. Multichannel marketing allows the vendor to sell more and at higher prices (Kumar and Venkatesan, 2005), although some other studies have tempered this trend based on the category of products (Kushwaha and Shankar, 2013). Digital channels have many major advantages: acquire new customers, develop sales with existing customers and reduce the cost of distribution of products. The acquisition of new customers can be achieved by stealing consumers from competitors, or by making new users want to consume (Kotler, Keller, 2012). As for developing sales with existing customers (that is, increasing the value of the average shopping basket), different techniques exist:

• **Nursing** involves enticing the internet or mobile user to make a second purchase immediately after having made a first purchase.

- **Cross selling** involves enticing the internet or mobile user to make a purchase which is complementary to the first.
- **Up-selling** involves encouraging the internet or mobile user to buy a more expensive product.

In general, digital media makes it possible to improve the shopping experience and thus to "push sales." Personalized offers generate trust and reinforce loyalty (to the brand and/or retailer). As reported by Khelladi et al. (2014), thanks to mobile devices, "companies can develop collaborative relationships to continually meet customer expectations and preferences." Finally, digital media allows for the reduction of distribution costs. Online retailers (pure players) do not need to invest in physical points-of-sale. Online shopping also enables a transparent inventory management, where stock levels are shared with the consumers in real-time. In short, mobile appears to be all-in-one. It is also one of the best tools to set up a CRM (Customer Relationship Management). Indeed, it delivers the following five elements: access to the consumer, knowledge of the consumer, dialogue with the consumer, building of emotions and finally, transaction.

For Smurtkupt et al. (2010), mobile marketing can serve the 4 elements of the Mix (the 4 "P"s, as well as the 4 "C"s), and even evolve them – as we have seen with LBS and **Product**. For Bissonnette and Brunelle (2014), it is up to the company to be "flexible without distorting their offering." On the **Pricing** side, mobile offers a possibility to increase profit: mobile devices can broadcast promotions. Victim of cognitive bias (Pham, 1996), the mobile user can be tricked by the feeling of getting an exceptional deal and therefore rush into buying without comparing prices offered by competitors. On the **Place** (Distribution) side (to which we will return), mobile can create traffic to the point of sale. Lastly, in terms of **Promotion** (another point to which we shall return), mobile phones allow us to target the consumer like never before. Mobile communication channels are effective: mobile email delivers a 65% open rate, according to Movable Ink (2015), text messages a 90% open rate, according to Oracle (2015) and push notifications are considered interesting by 70% of consumers who allow them according to Oracle (2015).

The consumer has never been so well-profiled and tracked. The probability of presenting relevant offers has never been so high. As for the 4 "C"s, here is the impact of mobile marketing on each of them:

- Consumer: the consumer can obtain useful and relevant information on demand

- Costs: a rational (see above) consumer can benefit from real-time deals.
- Convenience: mobile phones save time and energy for the consumer.
- Communication: the consumer is hyper-connected to the brand, but also to other consumers who can influence his attitude and behavior.
- We also must not forget the fact that the digital world can be an opportunity to refresh brand image. In the rationale of brand management (Aaker, 1996) and with the goal of building a strong brand, digital media can prove to be an effective weapon.

A "CHAMELEON CONSUMER"[27] IN TERMS OF ACCEPTANCE

In the post-modernist or even hypermodern logic, the consumer is not always rational. The consumer may, depending on various factors, choose to accept or not the intrusion of advertising. Rodriguez Goncalves, Pechpeyrou and Benavent (2014) note that "the contextual dimension will be one of the tracks to be explored to better explain variations in the degree of acceptance." Their recommendation is to choose opt-in strategies. This opt-in choice allows the consumer to retain control over the acceptance. For their part, Khelladi, Castellano and Limongi (2014)[28] state that for acceptance to be optimal, "location-based advertisements must be contextually valid." In summary, "individuals appreciate advertising messages that are informational, entertaining and tailored to their preferences."

On the contrary, advertisements which are perceived as unpredictable and uncontrollable, generate a strong sentiment of intrusion, resulting in an increase in anxiety and irritability (Khelladi, Castellano, Limongi, 2014). Therefore, while mobile is a very powerful medium for "push" strategies (directly addressing a message to the consumer, hoping to elicit a positive reaction), it must, nevertheless, be remembered that that "push" does not require a pre-approval from the customer. It is precisely for this reason that any marketer wishing to use this feature should do so sparingly and tactfully. Psychologically, there may be some roadblocks that would limit persuasion, due to the consumer refusing to accept such intrusive messages.

The ability for the consumer to be able to stop the flow of messages at any time is essential to prevent the risk of hurting the brand image.

The work of Edwards *et al.* (2002)[29] shows that the perception of intrusion is proportional to the degree of focus of the consumer during his internet brows-

---

27 Ernst & Young (2011), *Five New Consumer Trends*
28 Khelladi, I., Castellano, S., Limongi, L. (2014), *Revue française de marketing*, p. 43-58
29 Edwards, S.M., Li, H., Lee, J.-H. (2002), *Journal of Advertising*, 31 (3), p. 83-95

ing. In response to this intrusion, the consumer can put a defense strategy in place. He is then said to enter into resistance (Roux, 2014), whether through banner blindness (the consumer's disregard of advertising messages), or through the adoption of a negative attitude toward the message and the brand. A study conducted by OpinionWay (2016)[30] confirms the risk for a brand to develop a bad image in the mind of the consumer in 42% of respondents. In an exploratory study, Chouk and Guiot (2014) identify several consumer profiles according to this resistance:

- **Functional resistance** concerns internet experts. Their motivation to resist is based on their search for fluidity of navigation; advertising slows them down.
- **Ideological resistance** concerns individuals who refuse to accept this intrusion as it is an infringement on their personal freedom.
- **Cognitive avoidance** concerns a population that is not expert, but does not hesitate to leave the site if advertising is perceived as intrusive.
- **Non-resistance** concerns consumers who endure the intrusion as best they can, finding it to be normal, without any real means of counteracting it.

Leaving a consumer unsatisfied with his experience with the brand is a risk to said brand. The customer could switch brands, but above all, he could make himself the spokesperson of his discontent through negative word-of-mouth. In the digital age, word-of-mouth, such as online reviews, has become one of the most important sources of information for consumers. In a study conducted by DigitasLBI (2015), the influence of the opinions emitted on social networks is important. As a result, 39% of Facebook users believe that the platform affects the way they buy products[31]. It may seem irrational to trust anonymous individuals, but that is how the digital economy works. Bronner (2013)[32] wondered, "Why are we so gullible?" When applied to the internet, he proposes confirmation bias as an answer to his question; it happens when the individual has preconceived ideas for which he will find confirmation in the opinions of other internet users. In the end, these opinions give him confidence. Of course, this bias only works for the individuals who are superficially engaged, due to either a lack of knowledge or a lack of will. In this case, the quantity of opinions has an influence. In the opposite case, anonymous and weakly argued opinion has little influence on the confidence of a strongly engaged individual. The credibility of the reviews is reinforced under two conditions:

- Verified user, using personally identifiable information; and
- User reputation/rating.

---

30 OpinionWay (2016), *Study for Bonial*
31 Morgensztern, M. (2015), *e-marketing.fr*
32 Bronner, G. (2013), *Revue des deux mondes*, p. 85-94

In fact, according to Wathen and Burkell (2002)[33], the credibility of online information is based on a multitude of variables. It is not only a question of the credibility of the source (which is hardly ever known). It also includes the content of the message (objective and measurable arguments), the physiognomy of the site (ergonomics, design), as well as whether the reviewer is displaying an informed opinion (engagement and expertise). Sher and Lee (2009)[34] add a final element: the skepticism of the consumer. Thus, there would be two categories of individuals: those who are skeptic and who are therefore unlikely to be influenced by opinions and those who would be more inclined to pay attention to them. With regards to the anonymity of the source, which could prove detrimental to persuasion, it is not, in most cases, because this source represents a disinterested voice, at least officially. There is a great temptation for brands to interfere in the forums with fake reviews to counterbalance negative reviews (Mayzlin, 2006)[35]. According to several studies[36], these negative opinions tend to be more credible than positive ones in the mind of the consumer.

< FOCUS >

IPSOS LAUNCHES MEASUREMENT OF MOBILE CAMPAIGN EFFECTIVENESS

Ipsos is joining S4M, a mobile marketing specialist, to launch the first post-test to measure the impact of mobile advertising campaigns on branding. The efficiency of mobile media was until now, limited to the simple measurements of its performance (number of clicks, leads...). "The objective of this post-test is to go further in the ROI analysis of advertisers' investments, by measuring the effect of mobile marketing on brand image, as well as on the behavior of the consumer outside of the mobile device," explains Christophe Collet, president of S4M. In addition to advertising recall, this post-test helps to understand the impact on brand image, brand consideration and consumer alignment with the advertiser. The questionnaire also questions the mobile user on other media through which he could have seen the campaign, in an effort to assess the incremental contribution of mobile in a global media plan.

Source: Ipsos, 2016

---

33 Wathen, C.N., Burkell, J. (2002), *Journal of the American society for information science and technology*, p. 134-144
34 Sher, P., Lee, S. (2009), *Social behavior and personality*, 37, p. 137-143
35 Maizlin, D. (2006), *Marketing Science*, p. 155-163
36 Notably Lee, K.T., Koo, D.M. (2012), *Computers in Human Behavior*, p. 1974-1984

Since 2007, Publicis Eto publishes the *Intrusion Barometer*. In its fifth edition, published in 2015, several observations were made. First of all, it confirmed that consumers are "ambivalent." On the one hand, they perceive that the intrusion of brands into their personal lives is increasing daily, which bothers them (78% of the respondents) and, on the other hand, they are looking for services and deals, and willing to disclose information about themselves in exchange. Consumers are very reluctant about brands using data relating to their browsing outside the brand's digital ecosystem. More than 70% do not allow brands to access data from social networks. Finally, more than 73% do not agree that brands should retrieve geolocation information for commercial purposes.

At a high level, the main areas for improvement for m-commerce are ergonomics (mobile navigation is not the same as on a computer), payment (one-click options leveraging prerecorded payment details are particularly elegant) and trust, which is and remains core to the business. In digital commerce, trust is a more influential attribute than price. Indeed, the consumer can be reluctant to transact in a fully virtual environment. Best-in-class brands have built a reputation of the highest trustworthiness and benevolence.

According to Isaac and Volle (2014), the main trust-building criteria are based on several elements:

- Visibility of a strong brand;
- Prominence of the site's commitments to users (return policy, privacy policy);
- Secured payments, strong customer testimonials, and user path ergonomics.

But from an experiential perspective (i.e., a combination of tangible and irrational elements), the consumer bases her decision on her trust in the brand experience. This brand experience includes physical, sentimental, behavioral and intellectual dimensions. It does not require a physical consumption experience, but can remain in the imaginary stage. Some authors (Roederer, Filser, 2015) do not hesitate to speak in this context of a "meta-experience of the brand," i.e. a global experience of the brand, in the omnichannel context that the smartphone delivers.

Therefore, the question of privacy is central to the general adoption of digital marketing. While authors such as Baldi and Thaung (2002) consider that fun is the key success factor for mobile marketing, others emphasize non-intrusion into the private sphere (Barnes, Scornavacca, 2004[37]; Stuart, Eusebio, 2008[38]). In a literature review from Huang (2012)[39], respect for privacy comes first in the ranking of success criteria identified by researchers. Several models have been proposed by researchers, including that of Phelps, Nowak and Ferrell (2000)[40], as well as that of Malhora, Kim and Agarwal (2004)[41]. For the former, four factors should be considered:

- Type of personal data: a taste (say, a Facebook 'Like'), or a social security number or bank details.
- Level of control proposed by the site (from no control to full control).
- Potential benefits, such as saving time for shopping.
- Consumer characteristics, such as demographic data or attitudes toward marketing.

The latter proposes to look at data:
- Related to personal dispositions.
- Related to the context of the message receipt.
- Related to the individual (age, level of experience with internet, etc.).

The consumer may display unorthodox behavior. On the one hand, it seems that the consumer can express the greatest doubts and the utmost vigilance about attempts made by advertisers to intrude into their personal life. On the other hand, she shares personal information on her mobile, such as her banking data. This is called the "privacy paradox". One explanation for this phenomenon would be the "privacy calculus" (Culnan, 1995)[42]; that is, the consumer would make a calculated decision weighing the hope of gain and the risk of loss. This does not mean that the consumer is not concerned about the future of her data; she simply accepts it despite the risk.

37   Barnes, S. Scornavacca, E. (2004), *International Journal of Mobile Marketing*, 2, p. 128-139
38   Stuart, J.B., Eusebio, S. (2008), *International Journal of Mobile Marketing*, 6, p.405-416
39   Huang, R.Y. (2012), *International Journal of Mobile Marketing*, 7, p. 86-97
40   Phelps, J., Nowak, G., Ferrell, E. (2000), *Journal of Public Policy & Marketing*, Vol. 19, p. 27-41
41   Malhotra, N.K., Kim, S.S., Agarwal, J. (2004), *Information Systems Research*, Vol.15, p. 336-355
42   Culnan, M.J. (1995), *Journal of Direct Marketing*, Vol 9, p. 10-19

EXAMPLE

IDENTITY FRAUD PREVENTION IS A BUSINESS

Three types of tools have been launched on the identity protection market: anti-virus and data protection software that is installed on the mobile device, such as LookOut or Mobilelron; identity (and specifically credit score) monitoring tools, such as Experian or TransUnion; and insurances that cover identity theft – nowadays a common add on to many policies (offered by Geico, AllState, Axa and many others).

As Herault (2011)[43] notes, "individuals are increasingly concerned about the preservation of their privacy and companies' use of their personal data." This is precisely a source of differentiation for brands. Brands that appear to be more benevolent[44] and sensitive to this widely-accepted constraint may be more successful. It will depend on the importance that the consumer places (or chooses not to place) on the handling of his data.

In fact, everything depends on the sensitivity of the individual to their privacy. Westin (1996)[45] was the first to propose a typology of individuals according to their sensitivity to protecting their privacy. The first group (the "fundamentalists," 25% of consumers surveyed) is made of people who believe that citizens do not have sufficient control on their personal information and that the majority of businesses use this information in an abusive manner.

Individuals in the second group ("unconcerned," 20%), generally trust companies that ask them for personal information. Between these two extremes, "pragmatists" (55%) seek their own interest above all else. They analyze the proposed benefits along with the risks incurred and the guarantees offered, and then, they decide accordingly. Other work complemented Westin's. Spiekerman et al. (2001)[46] identify those who are "identity-concerned" (20%) as those who are concerned about having to provide personally identifiable information (name and email) and "profile concerned" (26%) as those who are concerned with socio-demographic and interest-based questions. Sheehan (2002)47, additionally, identified persons who were somewhat concerned about their privacy as "circumspect" (38%) and those who were very concerned about their privacy as "cautious" (43%).

43 Herault, S. (2011), *Actes du Colloque Medias* 011, p. 1-12
44 Gurviez, P., Korchia, M. (2002) *Recherches et Applications en Marketing*, Vol. 17, p. 41-61
45 Westin, A.F. (1996), *Equifax/Harris Consumer Privacy Survey*
46 Spiekermann, S., et al (2001), *Proceedings of the 3rd ACM conference on Electronic Commerce*, p. 38-47
47 Sheehan, B. (2002), *The Information Society: An International Journal*, Vol. 18, p. 21-32

< FOCUS >

REALIST CONSUMERS

- "On your mobile phone, you feel like you are being spied on." – 68% agree.
- "On your mobile phone, you are afraid of sharing information with brands without your knowledge." – 67% agree.
- "You feel like you are being invaded by brands on your mobile phone (too much spam)" – 60% agree.

Source: GFK "Mobile Marketing Consumer Report 2015".

In short, care must be taken to put in place a transparent data management policy, and educate the user on it. Publicis Eto concluded in its 2015 *Intrusion Barometer* that "the consumer needs more control over privacy management" (76.1% of respondents were interested in managing their own personal data through dedicated tools).

The essentials

· **In a digitalized world, everything would be within reach**. The consumer's happiness would be total. With the advent of the smartphone, she could buy when she wants, where she wants, at the pace she wants. Aided by mobile technologies and 360-degrees marketing technologies, brands and consumer would be very happy.

· **Yet this consumer is not completely fooled.** She suspects that in exchange for her immediacy expectations, there is a counterpart, which is intrusion. Though scrupulously regulated legally, the temptation is great for brands to dig into the habits and preferences of consumers. Therefore, beware of the blowback risk: consumer distrust of brands that would cross the Rubicon.

PART 2

ACQUISITION: A WINNING MOBILE CAMPAIGN

This section deals with strategic mobile marketing. While this medium is an integral part of digital marketing, it nevertheless has specific characteristics that the marketer must take into account. Based on immediacy and sharing of information, mobile is an unrivaled tool for advertising and sales efficiency.

CHAPTER 3
ECOSYSTEMS

Executive summary

Mobile marketing cannot be understood without understanding its ecosystems.

Major brands built an integrated value proposition for mobile users from hardware up to software, including browser, distribution or search engine. The entire value chain abounds with marketing and monetization possibilities.

These ecosystems can be understood vertically (as in the case of Apple or Google), or horizontally (as is the case with Samsung). They can be complete, like Apple, or partial, like Opera Software.

Keeping the "big picture" in mind is essential to daily mobile marketing needs. It provides a guiding tool to the marketer designing a mobile marketing campaign, developing its application offering, or trying to understand a newly created medium.

The proposed reading grid will help readers understand the uniqueness of Apple's brand, the sprawling grip of Google, Microsoft's difficulties in mobile, or Amazon's ambition.

The ecosystem model is unique by its simplicity of understanding and its resistance to the test of time.

The notion of ecosystem, nowadays overused, has a precise definition. It is borrowed from ecology and intends to describe "a system of interactions between populations of different species living in the same site, and between these populations and the physical environment," (Tansley, 1935). By extension, this notion will be used in economy.

James Moore (1996) attempts to describe a set or type of enterprises whose value is greater than the sum of the parts. The integration and synergies between these sub-sets themselves generate value. These co-evolve over time and tend to align themselves with each other towards the direction of a central enterprise.

It is in 2004 that the notions of verticality and horizontality of synergies between "heterogeneous actors guided by the promotion of a common resource and an ideology that will lead to the development of shared competences" appears in *The business ecosystems as a renewal of "collective strategies"* (Gueguen, Pellegrin, Torres (2005)[1].

Ecosystems contain a few key concepts: a common standard used by enterprises, the sharing of a common goal, the leading role of an enterprise that will guide the change, the integration of critical skills, the heterogeneity of actors (enterprises, institutions, manufacturers, and service providers), and the possibility of intra-systemic and extra-systemic competition.

The notion of ecosystem related to our subject resonates with this definition. For example, the Android ecosystem supports intra-systemic competition, where Samsung, Amazon and Google compete in the Android ecosystem. Only Apple meets a stricter, more "closed" definition. Indeed, created *ex nihilo*, its founder Steve Jobs wanted to build one with the sole purpose of creating quality and end-to-end control of the process. This non-competition, in the economic sense, is only possible insofar as all the parties are part of the same enterprise or include the same shareholders/managers, and, moreover, where a leader is charismatic or powerful enough to focus these energies in a single beam.

The reading grid proposed here offers a high-level vision and allows understanding of the movements of the telecom industry. From then on, the questions addressed are: Why does Google need to produce its own hardware? Why does Microsoft need devices beyond game consoles or virtual reality headsets?, and, Why is owning an App Store with a diversified offering also critical to selling hardware?

---

1 Gueguen, G., Pellegrin-Boucher, E. and Torrès, O. (2005), *The business ecosystems as a renewal of "collective strategies": the example of the software industry*

Apple's ecosystem as a market benchmark

The vertical ecosystem is understood as a silo. The energy of an entire enterprise is channeled to produce a complete, all-in-one product, a "one-stop shop" that meets all the needs of the end customer so that she has neither the necessity nor the desire to leave the perimeter of the enterprise's products. This ecosystem culture was born at Apple with the MAC, the personal computer that was first commercialized in 1984. As soon as technical possibilities were available (memory limit at 128 KB at the time), Apple proposed an Office suite and a printer. It is this logic that Microsoft subsequently implemented for the PC.

In the mobile sphere, Apple was immediately oriented towards an integrated offer. Firstly, because of its culture of control and quality. Secondly, because there was no credible digital and mobile offering at the time. It should be remembered that, in these days, the music industry was hit by Napster, LimeWire and others, and was unable to propose a legal alternative. iTunes put an end to this problem.

The iPhone ("a phone, a browser, a music player" as Jobs described it at the launch keynote in 2007), is built on this hardware and software basis. Jobs integrated the principle of applications (open the following year to external developers) and mobile browsing via the App Store and Safari. Today, Apple's integrated mobile offering looks like this:

9	Clients	1 billion active devices
8	Monetization	% on apps + in app, iAds, hardware sales
7	Payment	CC, prepaid cards, operator billing
6	Content & Distribution	AppStore (2 millions apps)
5	Browser	Safari
4	Search engine	Siri (+ Google, Y!, Bing)
3	Services	Mail, Cloud
2	Operating System	iOS (+ Mac OS, Apple TV OS, CarPlay)
1	Devices	iPod, iPhone, iPad, iWatch (+Mac, Apple TV)
	Brand	Apple

Source: Edosquet, Aurelie Guerrieri.

Table 3.1 – Apple's ecosystem

This diagram uses the OSI model and goes from the hardware layer to the software layers to the end client.

• The *device*, as we have seen, is an essential piece, strategic in more ways than one.

First, it is the support of the brand, the vector that the Apple tribe sports as a sign of recognition, socio-tribal tattoo, external sign of refinement and supposed social status. Additional stickers are even included in the brand's products' packages. Then, to control the device gives the certainty of maintaining the quality of the software products developed on it (memory, processor speed, and fundamental operating system ...), guaranteeing a rate of innovation, and controlling the timing of evolutions.

At Apple, timing is a key element of marketing. Each new product is presented at company keynotes, only available after a set waiting period, and before an intelligently orchestrated shortage. All this is benefits Apple's marketing.

Finally, the sales of Apple's hardware are a bounty. According to a study by iSupply (bought by Asymco), the hardware costs to manufacture an iPhone 4 are only $204, packaging $11, labor $15 (very little, especially in relation to the margin and the quality of life of the workers), and royalties $8 (even a closed and innovative system like Apple includes such costs). Add it all up and gross margin is about 58% and operating margin 51%! So, on a device sold for $600, the margin is about $300!

For more recent hardware, a study by Teardown.com provides some updates. The BOM (Bill of Materials), that is, the cost of assembled hardware, was only $ 227 for the iPhone 6 (sold for $ 760 in its 64 GB version), and $ 243 for the iPhone 6s (sold for $ 960 in its 64 GB version). In other words, Apple already has very large margins before even selling a single application on its App Store. According to reports released to its investors, Apple generated a little more than $32 billion of revenue on the iPhone for the last quarter of 2015.

The centers of profit, akin to business centers of gravity, are thus different between manufacturing silos: Apple has already earned profits from a device sale when Google has earned very little. Conversely, Apple generates very little revenue from the "search engine" aspect, which is the center of gravity for Google's ecosystem.

Revenues generated by iPhone sales are strategic in several ways. First, they absorb a significant part of the ARPU, eating from the share of wallet of competing brands. They increase the attractiveness of the stock price, in a competitive context. Finally, the generated cash flow makes it possible for Apple to protect itself from a number of unknowns, such as a major economic crisis (where recreational goods and services are the first to be impacted), or a technological failure (poor choice, inefficient technology) which could possibly be offset by the external acquisition of a more efficient solution.

Let us add that this is also a tactical advantage, which we will detail later: competitors have to purchase this element if it is not already part of their offer. This explains why Google had to pay $12.5 billion in 2011 to acquire Motorola. The operation was time consuming, affecting trust (Samsung, the Asian partner of Android felt betrayed) and cash consuming (Motorola had a negative operating margin), meaning that money was not available for other investments. In fact, Google withdrew from this acquisition in 2014: reselling it for only $3 billion in 2014, to Lenovo - a loss of a little less than $4 billion, excluding partial transfers and debts.

• The *operating system* (OS) is also a critical element in the value chain. It is the transmission belt between hardware and programs/applications/user interface. It is this element that allows for the optimization of key device purchasing factors, such as battery life, or processor speed. It is from this software layer that developers are able to code applications via the Software Development Kit (SDK).

The OS is therefore the base and the software core of the ecosystem. Applications must be adapted to each OS and to each OS version. Having a single OS, like Apple, is a major advantage as the community only needs to code once, and only make minor ergonomics improvements for the iPad, or iPad mini, for example. On Android, there are half a dozen OS versions and developers must ensure compatibility with each other, or assume losing a percentage of market share and risk disappointing the end customer.

The OS, as a user interface, is the visual signature of a product. It is from this element that the user experience will ultimately be determined. On iOS, you find the homepage, spotlight (search bar), status bar (battery, network), word processing features (copy, paste, etc.), camera, calendar, accelerometer, and/or multitouch.

Controlling the OS is controlling the capacity for innovation, competitive advantages and independence - in a word, the future. Analysts give iOS a market share situated between 20% and 25%, down sharply from the previous year, due to the fast growth of Android.

- **Services** are an important part of the package. They are normally included in the upper layers of the OS but, as part of an ecosystem comparison, it is worthwhile to elaborate. In fact, Apple communicated a great deal on these services as differentiating elements, especially at the beginning of the iPhone. The paradox is that this marketing was done on Google's account since two of its flagship services: YouTube and Maps (Google Maps), were highlighted. Apple began to substitute these services by its own offers. For example, Maps was replaced by an alternative community-based solution on the iPad3 *"open street map"*, then by Apple Maps.

  More recently, Apple has developed and communicated on its iCloud service, which backs up and synchronizes the contents of the iPhone, to a different device, which could even be a Windows PC. This offer, which is directly embedded in the device, does not require any complex manipulation and the storage space is free for up to 5 GB – note that this limit is low is today's world of rapidly decreasing storage costs.

- As much as hardware is the heart of Apple's business model, the **search engine** is the heart of Google's business model. Today, Apple and many other market players do not (yet) own search technology. There again, we have an illustration of how the ecosystem model predicts evolutions of the mobile industry.

  Today, three search engines are available on iOS through Safari: Google (default), Bing and Yahoo. Apple gets paid a percentage of the revenue generated by Google ads. The two actors are very closely linked by this synergy. Thus, Google accounts for 85% of mobile searches on Safari, Yahoo 9% and Bing a very small 1% (Source MarketShare hitslink). The remaining percentage points go to Chinese search engines such as Baidu, which are significant due China's rise in the world.

  An important element to understand is that Apple, thanks to revenue it generates elsewhere, is not dependent on Google. In fact, Google pays *a lot* of money to Apple; in January 2016, *The Guardian* revealed that Google paid Apple $1 billion to position Google as iOS's default search engine.

  So what is Apple's weapon to further its advantage in this aspect? The answer is clear: Siri. Firstly, Siri, a voice-based help tool, can be considered a search engine. To answer the question: "Find a Chinese restaurant on 8th avenue" Siri will run a search. Notably, the default search engine Siri uses is Microsoft's Bing. The form-factor is also interesting, insofar as it introduces the vocal dimension into the process. The user no longer needs to type text, making the user experience completely different and traditional methods obsolete. Siri offers everybody, including the illiterate 15% of the world population, people with disabilities, and a rapidly aging population, the opportunity to use its service. Another aspect currently being developed, Artificial Intelligence, will soon go so far as to anticipate the client's search, transforming Siri into a concierge-styled service. The future is here, it's within coding range, and it will be realized in a few years.

- The **browser** is an important element both in the generation of mobile traffic and in terms of monetization. Today, Apple has a product, Safari, but it is not a flagship. Why? Because there are better products on the mobile market, for example Opera Software with Opera Mini, which offers a very powerful tool, and is built by a firm at the origin of many Web standards, including CSS and HTML5.

Within closed systems such as Apple's, one can set several biases offering a massive market advantage. Indeed, though it's possible to configure the default search engine on iOS, it is *impossible* to remove Safari as the default browser. Thus, all queries launched from an app (in-app purchase, Twitter Web link, mobile web site link, etc.) will be from Safari, thereby educating and habituating the end user to it. Similarly, the browser launch icon is, by default, on the mobile home page, just next to the commonly used iMessage. Mozilla, an internet giant with 500 million downloaded PC browsers worldwide, has abandoned the idea of developing its mobile product, Fennec, on iOS – it's just not worth the investment to try and penetrate Apple's closed system.

- *Marketplace and applications.* Apple's revenue model is driven by hardware sales more than anything else, but the revenue generated by the App Store is still considerable. JP Morgan stated in a recent note that consumers of the App Store ("Appsumers") are being highly engaged in the ecosystem. Estimated App Store revenue for 2015 is $6.1 billion, including $1 billion during the holidays (gross margin after payment of 70% to developers). These revenues, when compared to the $32 billion generated by the iPhone alone in the last quarter of 2015, could be described as marginal for Apple, but would be positively gigantic to other firms.

- *Billing.* The subject is both simple and complex at the same time. It is simple because Apple has implemented the best solution for it and its customer: payment by credit card. This is the best solution for Apple because the merchant payout on a card is the highest among payment methods (around 98%), and simple for the customer because the payment method is linked to their iTunes account, meaning the user need only enter their password (or touch their fingerprint) to make a purchase.

It is complex because Apple, in order to support its growth and not leave an empty battle field to competitors, will have to seek customers in markets with low credit card penetration and with prepaid phone credits. However, there is a growing upper middle class in emerging markets such as the BRICs, that is attracted to Apple's more expensive devices. To some extent, Apple has already set up prepaid circuits for iTunes (in the form of cards that can be purchased at the supermarket), but it is too cumbersome of a user experience to significantly scale. That said, Apple *does* have the power to reverse a market: In a conference organized by Goldman Sachs in February 2012, Tim Cook convinced China Unicom to introduce postpaid plans for the iPhone by using the argument that the operator would have better control over experience and revenue, and that users would benefit from a cheaper service.

The Android ecosystem, hybrid model

Android is a hybrid system. It is used in its entire stack in devices marketed by Google (e.g. Nexus), and partially by a wide range of manufacturers throughout the world: European (Logicomm, Archos, Wiko), American (Dell) and Asian (LG, Samsung, Huawei, Alcatel, Lenovo, etc.)

Google's vertical stack is complete, even more so than Apple's. With the production of Nexus tablets and the Pixel phone, Google has a full proprietary offer, but continues to depend from partners for scale. The Android OS, of course, is one of the keys to its internal and external ecosystem. Note the Chrome OS, dedicated to tablets and laptops (*Chromebooks*), a shot across the bow to Microsoft. We have already detailed Google's many services, and the fact that they are free and ubiquitous is another very powerful element in its offerings. Google's search engine is at the heart of the ecosystem.

9	Clients	2 billion mobile customers/Android 80 % mobile market share
8	Monetization	% on apps+ in app, Adwords, AdSense, hardware
7	Payment	CC, Wallet, carrier billing, PayPal, prepaid
6	Content & Distribution	Google Play (2.3 million apps)
5	Browser	Chrome
4	Search engine	Google Search, Google Now
3	Services	Mail, Drive, Maps, YouTube, Photos, etc.
2	Operating System	Android, Android Wear, Brillo, Weave, Chrome
1	Terminals	Google Car, Nexus, Pixel, Chromecast, ChromeBook, Google Home, Daydream, Google Glass (defunct)
	Brand	Google

Source : Edosquet, Aurelie Guerrieri.

Table 3.2 – The Android ecosystem

Interestingly, Google has produced its own web browser (Chrome), not only to fill an empty space in a global portfolio, but to also serve as a basis for other services and products. Thus, the browser can be used as a basis for the OS (Chrome OS) on small hardware (netbooks, small tablets), and as an access ramp to remote services (Google docs) and storage spaces in the cloud. Here too, a well-calculated strategy is used to increase Google's value proposition, block the emergence of niches in emerging markets, and strengthen partnerships (or dependence, depending on the angle of view) with manufacturers. The last feature that makes the browser a key element and a backbone of Google's offer is the Chrome Web Store, which offers a game and application experience in the browser, adding a WebApps (today on desktop) element to the total package.

Let's add that owning the browser is a strong advantage in the technical control of online advertising. Indeed, Google offers ads based on clicks – so it is fundamental to be able to propose the most appealing banners and texts to its internet users. To do this, it is necessary to be able to analyze either cookies or browser history, which is much easier to do if you control this element.

Today, the market share of Android (OS) ranges, according to analysts, between 65% and 80% of mobile and tablet traffic compared to 55% a year earlier. Chrome's market share is 55% compared to 38% for the previous year. The market share of the search engine is 95%, stable year to year.

Google's ecosystem is hybrid. We have just described it in its verticality, it is also horizontal – i.e., open to any platform for "free" (except for royalties). It's a tremendous springboard for any manufacturer who wants to enter the mobile race at a low cost and in a short period of time. The proposal is enticing because it avoids mobilizing significant R&D capital to develop an OS (and a whole ecosystem,) and relieves marketing of the need to compete with Apple directly.

But is the financial logic compatible with the industrial strategy? Has the "Financial Quarter" logic become the enemy of the decennial vision that allows investors to invest in breakthrough technologies that can change market share significantly? Can we regard this alliance as a Faustian pact whose actors would have been rewarded with an immense technological power at the cost of their souls as innovators? In exchange for Android, Google controls the monetization of the ecosystem, arguably downgrading its partners to the rank of simple manufacturers.

Does Google not keep the most qualitative part of the business from its Android partners? Isn't the short-term benefit to them low in light of the medium-term disadvantages? To what extent can manufacturers differentiate among themselves? How will they be able to build their own identity by embarking on the same products and services? What will they be able to do when Google decides to reserve certain features, or exclusive competitive advantages, to its own devices?

Alternative ecosystems, the resistance is getting organized

In a walled-off world where a duopoly dominates the market, how is it possible, if not to break through the walls, at least to survive? In recent years, market players have reorganized and restructured themselves to try to increase their footprint. Some even tried to be part of the action rather than the reaction.

At this stage, the market can be modeled as follows (Table 3.3).

SAMSUNG

Samsung tried to gain independence from Google, by producing a system called BADA, then Tizen, and promoting it, the more so than Google, via the purchase of Motorola, had become a competitor and not only a partner.

The principle of the Tizen ecosystem can be qualified as a simplified vertical one. It is vertical because it is not shared with other manufacturers. It is simplified because it does not integrate an offer as complete as that of Apple or Google.

The difficulty in promoting an ecosystem lies in the ability to attract developers to the operating system. Most often, the economics of large publishers do not allow for developing beyond two OS, in this case Android and iOS. The installed Tizen base (and the logic is the same for Windows mobile) is not large enough to amortize production costs. Samsung tried to reach a critical threshold by financing developments on its OS but the program failed. The invisible hand of the market will not let itself be forced.

MICROSOFT (AND NOKIA)

It would be easy to mention only Microsoft here. Microsoft acquired the device part of Nokia in September 2013 for $7.2 billion, consolidating a relationship the two firms had entered into just a few years earlier, in a symbiotic logic where Nokia provided the devices (e.g. the Lumia range), some services such as "Here", and the browser service, while Microsoft provided the foundation for the ecosystem, namely the OS (Windows 7 and Windows 10), a marketplace and a "cross-device" continuity of experience between the PC, the game console and mobile.

The merger cannot be considered a success. From a human point of view, the American culture did not necessarily correspond to the Finnish one. 15,000 people from Nokia were fired in 2014, affecting the motivation, brains and culture that had made the company a success. Victims of this wave of firings even ended up developing a competitive device (Jolla) and OS (SailfFish). Then, Microsoft was unable to attract a critical mass of developers to encourage the consumer to enter its ecosystem. The lack of applications offered on the Microsoft's Marketplace did not allow sales to take-off. In fact, only a year later, the company depreciated the acquisition of Nokia in fiscal year by $7.6 billion, in addition to a restructuring cost of $850 million!

Today, the market share of Windows phone is 0.7%, compared with 2.5% for the previous year. The share of Internet Explorer is 2%, down slightly from the previous year, while Bing, the search engine, is at 1%, where Yahoo, not in a brilliant shape itself, has around 3% of market share. Not surprisingly, Microsoft announced in May 2016 the abandonment of the production of mobile devices.

AMAZON

In fine, Amazon has been the most successful in creating a complete ecosystem. Even though the Fire phone was abandoned one year after its launch, Amazon has capitalized on the success of its Kindle Fire tablets to distribute its contents on its own App Store (we'll detail this in later chapters) in a synergistic manner that rewards Amazon's best customers, Prime subscribers.

Amazon offers a specific Android OS for services, a browser (Silk), an App Store, a one-click payment system, which has payment information stored for hundreds of millions of customers, and a voice-operated ordering system, Alexa.

Amazon represents the "third way" of the eco-systemic business model. Apple is paid for the hardware, Google for advertisement, and Amazon gets paid for sales of products and apps. These are the bases of the DNA of these companies. Apple makes beautiful products, Google monetizes its search engine, and Amazon sells over and over again (and reinvests all of its profits in research, logistics, robotics, and space exploration).

9	Clients	Windows Mobile: 1.1% market share	1.2 m smartphones sold (99% with android)	320 million Amazon accounts	200 million active users	500 million active users
8	Monetization	% on apps+ in apps, Bing Ads, hardware license	Hardware sales	% on apps+ in apps, content sales	App sales, services, advertising	License, % search, % apps sales
7	Payment	CC, new MS Wallet, carrier billing, Paypal	Google payments	CC, Amazon payment, Carrier billing, Paypal	Opera payment exchange, carrier billing	Carrier Billing
6	Content and Distribution	Windows store (660 thousand apps)	Google play, Tizen store	Amazon appstore Amazon Underground	Opera appstore	Firefox marketplace
5	Browser	Edge/Internet Explorer	« Samsung internet » Chrome	Silk	Opera browser Desktop, opera mini, opera TV	Firefox
4	Search engine	Bing, Cortana	Android search (Google search, Google Now)	Alexa	Google search, Y!, Bing	Google search, Y!, Bing
3	Services	Mail, office, Maps, Skype	Android services	Cloud, Amazon Video,	N/A (mail service closed)	Mail (Thunderbird)
2	Operating System	Windows mobile	Android, Tizen	Fire OS (based on Android)	N/A	Boot2Gecko, Firefox OS
1	Terminals	Lumia, Surface, Surface Pro, Surface Book, Hololens, Xbox	Galaxy, Gear, Tab, S line, etc	Fire Phone (abandoned), Fire tablet, Echo, TV, Dash	N/A	Abandoned

Source : Edosquet, Aurelie Guerrieri.

Table 3.3 – The alternative ecosystems

The model as a reading grid

If considering the ecosystem model as predictive, it would be possible to use it as a framework for decoding and anticipating a certain number of movements in this market segment.

Facebook is an interesting topic in this regard. Indeed, the firm has everything to position itself as an eco-systemic actor. Firstly, Facebook capitalizes on a phenomenal movement with more than one and a half billion users, of which more than half are on mobile. It has also skillfully maintained relationships with manufacturers and operators delighted to see their mobile traffic increase via Facebook. Manufacturers have already produced devices with a Facebook button (e.g. HTC Chacha). We have heard rumors about the production of a Facebook device (still denied by the Menlo Park firm), but nothing would prevent the launch of such a product.

The OS can be taken off the shelf with Android. The App Store and entertainment experience have already been in place and running since the early years of the platform. As for the monetization aspect, it is the heart of Facebook, a free service, with revenues of $27 billion (and profits of $10 billion) in 2016.

The takeover of WhatsApp for some $19 billion could be understood as the integration of a messaging service, the trajectory of which could have prejudiced Facebook. However, WhatsApp offers messaging, file-sharing and calling services. In a sense, Facebook is already a virtual telecom operator albeit without a SIM card.

But the physical support of Facebook may not need to be a tablet, or a mobile, since the firm founded by Zuckerberg is already present on those devices. Facebook is one of the most downloaded apps in the world. Other supports can be invested in, such as Oculus Rift, acquired in 2014 for $2 billion.

Beyond this eco-systemic model, a myriad of niche players has emerged, notably in mobile marketing, allowing an understanding of users' habits and consumption patterns. The key point to understand here is that innovation today comes less often from big players, like Apple or Google, than from startups born out of the big bang that was initiated precisely by these major brands.

The quality of the products and services offered by this group is also radically refined and complex. This is no longer a question of putting publishers and advertisers in touch with each other, but of bringing big data and artificial intelligence technologies into play. This is the subject of the next chapters.

The essentials

- **Major brands** mainly develop an integration strategy that is horizontal, total or partial.

- **The term ecosystem** refers to a set of precise definitions derived from biology or economy. We speak of symbiotic interactions and of the integration of parts whose value is greater than the sum of the parts.

- **These ecosystems** can be horizontal or vertical, complete or partial, closed or open.

- **Apple** has a 20% market share but captures 80% of the value.

- **In terms of OS**, we are in a situation of duopoly between iOS and Android. Microsoft accounts for only 1% to 2% of the market share. Even Samsung, a financial, marketing and technical giant, is unable to impose an alternative OS.

- **The number of applications available** on an App Store is directly correlated to the number of devices sold.

CHAPTER 4
MOBILE CAMPAIGN STRATEGY

Executive summary

· **Mobile marketing** opens up potential for immense success and innovation, and an opportunity to get ahead of the competition.

· **Indeed, on average, companies** underfund mobile marketing budgets.

· **Moreover, it's a 'winner takes all' world,** because minutes spent on mobiles are concentrated on a small number of mobile sites and applications.

The growth of mobile marketing budgets is dazzling. In September 2015, eMarketer predicted that mobile marketing would account for 25% of digital marketing in 2017. With media growth not showing signs of slowing down, thanks to video and social networks, in June 2016, Zenith, a subsidiary of the Publicis group, author of the report "Advertising Expenditure Forecast," updated the forecast for 2017. The global mobile advertising market will represent nearly $100 billion and more than half of digital marketing budgets.

Two strong trends in media consumption come together to reinforce the inevitable expansion of mobile marketing. On the one hand, Mary Meeker (2016) shows that the percentage of time spent on mobile is higher than the marketing budget allocated to mobile:

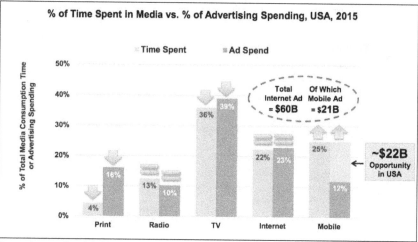

Source: *Internet Trends 2016*, KPCB, Mary Meeker.

Figure 4.1 – Percentage of time spent by media vs. advertising spend (US) in 2015

On the other hand, App Annie shows that the number of popular properties on mobile is drastically smaller than the number of popular properties on desktop.

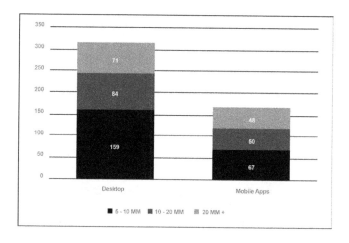

Source: App Annie (Apps), comScore (desktop), June 2015, US

Figure 4.2 – Number of websites vs. mobile applications having reached 5, 10 and 20 million unique visitors

To be part of these chosen few, one must develop an effective mobile marketing strategy.

Understanding and identifying targets

The first step in setting up a marketing campaign is to define the ideal user's profile. The more accurate the definition of this profile is, the more efficient the customer acquisition program will be in targeting and generating high lifetime users. Standard demographic criteria aren't sufficient in mobile marketing. Generally, relevant factors include:

- **Demographics**, such as gender, age, geographic location, education, income, and others.
- **Mobile behaviors**, such as device, number of applications used per day, time of use, click-through or purchase frequency.
- **Areas of interest** related to offered products or services.
- **Degree of loyalty**: different behaviors used to define loyalty and commitment of an application's user.
- **Purchase path**: desired actions after the installation of the application by a new user.
- **Lifetime**: knowing the average lifetime of users helps pay out the optimal price at each stage of their acquisition.

After defining target users, it is necessary to set the objectives of the campaign: Is it to generate installations, *in-app* purchases, or maybe to deepen the engagement of your users?

Once objectives are defined, one must establish corresponding performance expectations so that all stakeholders and partners can develop a program that achieves the expected results and remains affordable.

Take for example the mobile games industry. Developers often use performance-based campaigns that contribute to achieving business objectives and profitability.

This is especially common for *free-to-play* games (called *"freemium"*), such as *Candy Crush,* whose business model is exclusively geared towards in-app purchases. Their marketing strategy is based on contracting with performance marketing partners, who drive the acquisition of users that download the app, with the end goal of making *in-app* purchases.

< FOCUS >

CANDY CRUSH'S RECIPE FOR SUCCESS

There are almost 100 million people who play this game every day and more than 320 million different people play each month. The game is free; one only pays for small extras. Those extras don't cost much each time. It is painless and easy to pay, because your credit card is already saved in your Smartphone or with your operator. The advantage for the developer is that, once the game becomes popular, they do not have much left to do. They must maintain interest and develop new worlds or levels, but manufacturing or distribution costs are very low. Even if less than 5% of players spend a few cents, the game becomes a cash machine. For example, King Digital has $2 billion in sales and $825 million in profits.

Source: Les Échos, March 2014.

From guerrilla to all-out marketing war

Once the application is developed, it must be tried out by potential users in order to test it and to begin fueling the word-of-mouth machine. This is a critical phase because it will help to bring about necessary improvements through feedback collection and the observation of users' behavior. It also allows for earning the loyalty of the first hundred of users and collecting the first reviews in the App Store. During this phase, the finalization of the application's graphic charter also happens, starting with the choice of its icon in the App Store.

From a marketing point of view, this phase should be focused on free marketing channels: this is what is known as "guerrilla marketing." The app needs to be present on social networks; a Facebook page is the minimum. The other social networks are to be explored depending on the type of application and the targeted consumer. For example, a person-to-person fashion sales application, such as Poshmark, must be very active on Instagram and highlight the visual content created in the application by posting photos. Similarly, a news application, such as News Republic, will choose Twitter to connect with existing channels relevant to its target and topics. Finally, a marketer can simply participate in existing conversations on social networks and mention the name of her application. Let us not forget that most of the social media's consumption happens via mobile. It, therefore, represents an ideal platform to target the intended population.

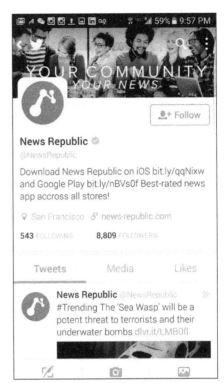

Figure 4.3 – Poshmark on Instagram   **Figure 4.4–News Republic on Twitter**

It is sagacious to embed a viral mechanism within the application. For example, the social network Secret was only available at the beginning by invitation, and the mysterious content of the shared secrets created a high demand for these invitations. One can also create a waiting list, fictitious or not, to exacerbate this effect. Of course, users will often be reminded to share the application, or the content of the application, with their network.

The objective of opening all the free distribution channels is, on the one hand, to prime the machine, because word of mouth takes time to amplify, and, on the other hand, to collect valuable user feedback before spending fortunes on marketing and facing a potential fiasco.

After a few weeks, the phase of paid marketing can begin.

Every major marketing launch is preceded by a pre-launch which aims to:

- Anticipate possible bugs.
- Gain feedback from users.
- Accumulate positive comments in the App Store.
- Fine-tune both the application and its presentation.

Large developers[1] generally carry out this launch in a country with a common language and a smaller population. An American developer, for example, will launch a new application in Canada or Australia before launching it in the US market. This is the case of Gameloft who sees these countries as representative tests of the king market, the US market.

A new objective is added to the previous one in this phase: to test marketing strategies and measure their effectiveness. The following paragraphs will explain how.

Then comes the full launch, and here, marketing budgets can be unlimited! The freemium gaming sector is one of the most competitive. New games are launched every day, and the only way to stand out is by getting ranked on the suggestion lists of the App Stores, that is to say, among the apps that are the most downloaded. The big developers are fighting to rank in the top ten sales in each country and stay there. Some like MachineZone (which publishes Mobile Strike), Supercell (Clash of Clans), King.com (Candy Crush) spend hundreds of millions of dollars per year for this purpose. For example, in 2014, Supercell spent over $400 million in marketing and King.com over $450 million[2].

---

1 Eric Seufert
2 GamesBrief

< FOCUS >

THE POKÉMON MADNESS

In the summer of 2016, the Pokémon Go madness took hold of the mobile world. From New York to Taiwan, from Sweden to Australia, Pokémon breeders ran the streets, even reaching a Norwegian representative who was playing during a parliamentary session.

It was a unique phenomenon. This application's ability to go viral teaches us something by becoming a reference, a master standard of word of mouth, and of how a single application can impact the stock price of its publisher.

According to the firm App Annie, the number of active players rose from 0 to 45 million in two weeks in July, with users even downloading the application illegally in countries where it was not yet available. The drop off was about 30% by the end of the summer.

By the same token, Nintendo's shares, publisher of the application, rose from 14,500 yen to 31,700 yen between the 1st and the 19th of July before stabilizing at around 28,000 by summer's end.

Apple, via its App Store, is also one of the beneficiaries of this madness.

The investment bank Needham & Co estimates their gain at close to $3 billion in 12-24 months via the 30% "cut" taken on in-app purchases.

In a tweet dated August 3rd and not by chance, Tim Cook, CEO of Apple, celebrated the month of July 2016 as the most profitable since the creation of the App Store.

How can we explain that word of mouth success?

- The Pokémon brand was already well established worldwide. Founded in Japan in 1998, The Pokémon Company generated between $1.5 and $2.5 billion annually from licenses via video games, cartoons, and films.
- Innovation through virtual reality. Developed by Niantic Labs, a company whose investors counted Google before Nintendo joined in; the technology aims to include the characters of the game in the players' physical reality.

- The materiality of the community. Playing outdoors, fans met each other in parks, public transport or their workplaces. Thus, cooperation and competition, sometimes spectacular and in front of other people, allowed this game to benefit from a word of mouth which itself generated a full media buzz in the calm summer before the saturation of the Olympic Games.

Basic definitions.... and complex solutions

A paid mobile marketing campaign includes at least the following 4 elements:

- A budget.
- A duration.
- At least one visual.
- At least one media placement.

MOBILE CAMPAIGN STRATEGY

Mobile marketing campaigns can be billed as follows:

- CPM - Cost Per 1,000 impressions.
- CPC - Cost Per Click.
- CPI - Cost Per Installation.
- CPA - Cost Per Acquisition. For example, an account creation on OpenTable.
- CPS - Cost Per Sale. For example, the first purchase on Amazon.
- CPL - Cost Per Lead. For example, a user who gave his / her name and address in a home improvement search application.
- CPE - Cost Per Engagement. For example, a player who has reached the 3rd level of a game application.
- CPV - Cost Per View. Exclusively for video format, it refers to paying for each viewed video.
- CPCV - Cost Per Complete View. Exclusively for video format too, but it is about paying for each fully viewed video.

Each purchase order must define precisely the billing mode, the measurement tool used, as well as the procedure in case of disagreement on the amounts.

Media Logo									
I.O. #: XYZ123						Typical Insertion Order			
Date 6/7/2017									

Advertiser
Name and address
Name, email and phone number of contact person

Financial Contact
Name and address
Name, email and phone number of contact person

Agency
Name and address
Name, email and phone number of contact person

Financial Contact
Name and address
Name, email and phone number of contact person

Publisher
Name and address
Name, email and phone number of contact person

Financial Contact
Name and address
Name, email and phone number of contact person

Campaign	Target age	Target geo	Target gender	Start date	End date	Cost per unit	Quantity	Unit	Total cost
TopApp - 320x50	18-25	US, DE, UK	F	6/8/2017	7/20/2017	1.50	20,000	CPI	30,000
TopApp - video	18-25	US	F	6/15/2017	Open ended	3.50	1,000	CPI	3,500
TopApp – native messages	18-25	US	F	6/21/2017	6/21/2017	4	1,000	CPI	4,000
									37,500

Special instructions
Attribution tool: xyz
Daily cap : 100 installs

Terms and conditions
Link to master agreement, terms and conditions, and privacy policy -- as applicable.

Advertiser or Agency

By : _____

Name
Title
Date

Publisher

By: _____

Name
Title
Date

Table 4.1 – Typical insertion order "I.O."

MOBILE CAMPAIGN STRATEGY

In addition, consider user targeting options. Depending on the platforms and marketing partners, as well as the advertiser's own data, these options may vary significantly. The major categories are based on:

- Demographics:
  - Age, gender.
  - Location (from country to zip code, or city).

- Psychographics:
  - Socioeconomic categories.
  - Hobbies, such as travel, finance, and games.
  - Activities such as social networks, photography, and more.

- Mobile behavior:
  - Apps used recently and/or frequently.
  - Apps present on the telephone.
  - Recently visited websites.

- Temporal:
  - Frequency: maximum number of times per day and/or per campaign the user is exposed to the ad.
  - Programming: hours of the day and days of the week when the campaign is visible.
  - Mode of expenditure of the budget: spent immediately or distributed during the day or the campaign period.

- Mobile:
  - Brand and model of the telephone; Smartphone or tablet.
  - Operating system (Android, iOS) and its version.
  - Telecom operator.
  - Connectivity mode (Wi-Fi or 3G for example).

FACT SHEET

AVOIDING SCAMS

Each measurement unit has its faults and weaknesses. Here is how to recognize and mitigate them:

· CPM: Impression fraud is relatively easy and very lucrative. Forensiq, a verification company, estimates that more than 30% of programmatic mobile impressions are potentially fraudulent[3]. It is possible to use robots to simulate an ad view, or to hide ads one below the other or at the bottom of the pages so that they are invisible to users. To remedy this problem, a basic measure is to require screen-shots of real placements and to go on one's mobile and surf that media to find one's ads. To limit more sophisticated fraud, one should require the use of a veri-fication tool, which will confirm when the ad is completely downloaded and vis-ible to the user by sending a signal.

· CPC, CPI, CPA, CPL, CPE: Fraud is generated by the use of robots. The closer the performance measurement is linked to user behavior, the harder it is for robots to

---

3 MediaPost

imitate a real user. Therefore, there is more fraud in CPC models than CPE ones. To detect virtual users, companies use signal combinations that can include IP address, user behavior analysis over time, user agent, and more.

· CPS models are the most difficult to trick because they require creating fraudulent means of payment for these fake users. Often, the gain is not worth the effort. However, when this is not the case, sophisticated scams can be developed, such as the one Uber fell victim to in China (see the following example)[4].

< FOCUS >

UBER SCAMMED IN CHINA?

China was a huge market for Uber, and before exiting it, they faced serious local competitors, such as Didi Kuaidi, and international ones, such as Lyft. In an effort to recruit drivers, Uber promised them a bonus for each trip, which was sometimes far greater than the price of the trip.

A parallel market of Uber accounts was created on the TaoBao e-commerce platform, where fake drivers could meet fake passengers and make "empty" journeys for which they were paid. Tencent estimates the fraud involved more than one million trips. One can imagine that the profitability of the corresponding marketing campaign was not one of the best...

THOMAS BOUTTEFORT
Co-Founder, SHAPR

WHAT IS SHAPR?

Shapr is the "Tinder" of network-ing. Every day, we offer a selection of people to meet based on multi-ple criteria. Our mission is to ensure that our users meet individuals who can change their lives or at least get them out of their daily lunch routine. The application was launched in Sep-tember 2014 on iOS and Android, and we are in a growth phase, that is to say, a phase of user acquisition and strong growth since October 2015. In the summer of 2016, we had an install base of 100,000 users, of which 70% were in the United States, mainly in New York and Los Angeles. San Fran-cisco was launched at the beginning of 2016.

The specific nature of our product means that our marketing tactic is to "launch" cities and not countries. We must ensure that our users who share common interests are in prox-imity and can actually meet each other easily. We target 500,000 users by the end of 2017.

HOW DO YOU ADDRESS GROWTH PROBLEMS?

Growth is in our DNA. We think of it like we think of agile development.

There is no absolute golden rule and nothing routine about user acquisi-tion. In growth, there is no silver bul-let; we have to test on cycles that are sometimes very short, e.g. one day, to identify and validate optimal acquisi-tion patterns.

Traditional branding remains key for an industry like ours. It drives organic traffic and reengagement.

Balanced scaling of the quantita-tive and qualitative sides is key. It is useless to acquire hundreds of thou-sands of users if they do not fully en-gage with the application. We seek increased engagement over raw us-er counts.

The essentials

· **The first step** in setting up a marketing campaign is to understand and identify the target customer, and define the campaign's objectives: is it to generate installations, *in-app* purchases, or maybe to deepen the engagement of your users?

· **The marketing plan** must begin with a guerilla or word-of-mouth phase to test the application in the real world and get feedback. Then, it shall include a test in a small, representative country. Finally, marketing campaigns are ready for large-scale expansion, which in some cases can be enormous, and reach hundreds of millions of dollars.

· **A paid mobile marketing campaign** includes at least the following 4 elements: 1) a budget, 2) a duration, 3) at least one visual, and (4) at least one media placement. In addition, one should consider user targeting criteria.

· **Watch out for fraud!** The wild wild west side of mobile marketing makes it a fertile ground for scams.

CHAPTER 5
MARKETING OBJECTIVES

Executive summary

Acquiring new users is one of the most frequent objectives of marketing campaigns because even the best applications need marketing to distinguish themselves in an ocean of hundreds of thousands of available apps.

Fierce competition for the fleeting attention of mobile users focuses mobile marketing efforts on acquiring users who will continue to use the app every day.

The app world

It is no longer reasonable to believe that an app could grow and scale without a marketing budget. That is far from being the case, no matter how high the quality of the app.

Example: Let's take the free game *Ninja Kid Run* by Fun Games. It has garnered over 2,500 user reviews and an average rating of 4.5 stars. Impressive! Its users leave over-the-top reviews ("I love this app," "best game there is," etc.)

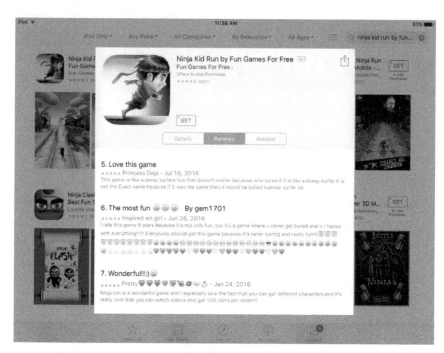

Figure 5.1 – Ninja Kid Run: Reviews

A real success, right? Unfortunately, look at the ranking that this game has: 81st on the list:

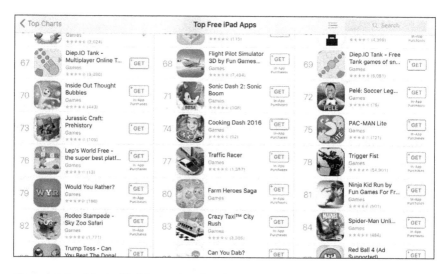

Figure 5.2 – Ninja Kid Run: Ranking

So, even a great app like *Ninja Kid Run* has no hope of breaking the top charts without a solid marketing push.

Does this hold true at the macroscopic level, across all categories? AppAnnie demonstrates how elite the winners' circle is: the typical user spends over 20 minutes per day on a single app! New entrants vying for attention are competing for a fraction of the available media time.

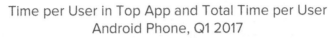

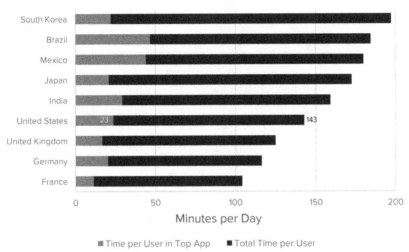

Figure 5.3 – Percentage of time spent on top app vs all apps
Often times, the top app will be a messaging or a social app. But not all social apps can aspire to the top spot. The largest ones are also the ones with the deepest engagement, creating a seemingly impenetrable virtuous cycle of usage:

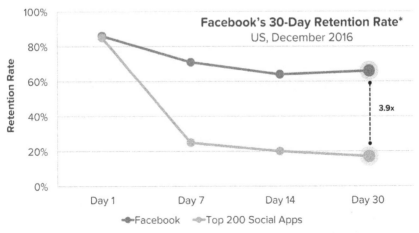

Source: App Annie, Android, US, December 2016

Figure 5.4 – Facebook user retention rate compared to other top social apps

As soon as she turns her phone on, the user is exposed to and engaged by her favorite applications, relegating other apps to the deeper abysses of the confines of her smartphone. She even forgets some applications she's downloaded.

Which applications attract attention? App Annie demonstrates that the 10 most popular apps of all time have all been created during the large population wave of the App Store in 2008-2012. Even then, we know that most of them have had to spend significant marketing dollars in recent years.

In a world where even the best of applications cannot stand out from the crowd solely on their own merits, but require significant marketing campaigns, mobile marketing for user acquisition has become an essential component for any developer. *Business Insider* estimated the market for mobile app installation advertising to top $5 billion in the US in 2016.

Top Apps by Downloads
iOS & Google Play, US, 2012 - 2016

Rank	App	Company	Release Date*	Country of Headquarters
1	Facebook Messenger	Facebook	August 2011	United States
2	Facebook	Facebook	July 2008	United States
3	Instagram	Facebook	October 2010	United States
4	Pandora Radio	Pandora	July 2008	United States
5	Snapchat	Snap	July 2011	United States
6	Netflix	Netflix	April 2010	United States
7	YouTube	Google	December 2011	United States
8	Skype	Microsoft	March 2009	United States
9	Candy Crush Saga	Activision Blizzard	November 2012	United States
10	Spotify	Spotify	July 2011	Sweden

*Earliest release date on either app store

Figure 5.5 – Ranking of the all-time most popular applications
Far from the "land grab" marketing of the beginnings of the App Store, where any expense was justified to acquire the *most* users in a minimum of time, today's fierce competition for the scarce attention of mobile users focuses mobile marketers' efforts towards acquiring the *right* users: those who will continue to use the application, day after day.

It is therefore necessary to understand the desired user behavior prior to any investment in mobile media, and to define key performance objectives to be measured during the campaign: the KPIs, or Key Performance Indicators.

There are two scenarios, each with a different set of KPIs to monitor:

- The app is paid.
- The app is free.

Paid applications often include utilities (such as the Swiftkey keyboard, Lookout antivirus, or Evernote note-taking), business applications or games (such as the global success story, *Angry Birds*). With paid apps, it is essential to hone in on the optimum price: that which maximizes income, that is to say, the highest price that can be afforded before discouraging potential buyers. This is the Revenue per Installation (RPI). This ideal price can be established by testing different price points on the App Store and measuring corresponding sales and user lifetime value (defined later). One can also guess the psychologically acceptable price by studying potential users in focus groups. However, as a rule, the paid app model has been less popular than the free app model.

In the case of the free model, the developer monetizes the app through a combination of advertising and in-app purchases (IAP). As a result, total income accumulates with each additional usage of the application by each user. The Average Revenue Per User (ARPU) will vary according to the lifetime of the user and her depth of engagement with the application.

The lifetime is the duration during which the user will use the application on a regular basis - on average, less than 4 months for a mobile game[1]. At the end of this time, the user grows tired of the application and either uninstalls it, or simply forgets about it.

The user's journey, at the time of each use, defines the advertisements to which she will be exposed, as well as the opportunities and the probability of purchase. On the advertising side, it is necessary to calculate an average revenue per placement, depending on the size of the advertisement, the type of visual, its position in the user flow, the user's device and operating system. For example, in a game, an award-winning video can earn more than $15 CPM for users on iOS, while a footer banner will yield less than $1 CPM for users of the same game on Android.

---

1 Flurry, 2013

Optimizing in-app purchases is a matter of art and science. To put it simply, let's consider a mobile game, such as Supercell's *Hay Day*. In this game, the probability of purchase is strongly correlated to the game play. First, to hook users, they are led to progress easily in the game without having to pay a penny. For example, at the start of the game the user is given a farm with some seeds. She can easily meet the challenges of planting and harvesting and from that moment on, compete with other farmers. Then, as she becomes hooked, the difficulty of each level increases, and she will be offered the possibility of overcoming these difficulties by buying bonuses: accelerating the growth of seeds, purchasing land, requesting assistance from other farmers, and so on. At this point, many users will drop out, and use the game less and less. But our "addicted" user will not find it difficult to spend $ 1.99 to advance in the game. A small number of them will spend fortunes (commonly hundreds of dollars or more). They will become what are called "whales," who are much sought after as the best consumers.

The challenge for the application developer is to identify these profitable consumers from their first visit on, in order to guide marketing strategy, without having to wait months to measure their value. Each application developer must create a LifeTime Value (LTV) model that places each cohort of users on a potential revenue curve. The LTV is based on 3 main factors:

- **Monetization:** What users spend over the life of the application. ARPDU (Average Revenue Per Daily User), ARPPU (Average Revenue Per Paying User) and ARPU (Average Revenue Per User) are some KPIs.
- **Retention AND engagement:** This measures the frequency and rate at which users re-open the application, what they do, and how long they stay there.
- **Virality:** this is the number of incremental users that this user will bring for free. Virality is best measured over a certain length of time.

Each developer will create a secret LTV calculation formula, based on the variables of each of these categories.

FACTSHEET

CALCULATING THE RETURN ON INVESTMENT (ROI)

Return on investment is defined as the sum of revenues minus the sum of costs, divided by the sum of revenues. But it is more interesting to measure it at the level of each campaign, as it is a measure of their effectiveness.

For each marketing campaign, a cost per installation (CPI) can be calculated by taking the sum of the costs and dividing it by the sum of the installations. By comparing it with the ARPU or the RPI defined above, one obtains the ROI:

ROI = (RPI - CPI) / RPI or ROI = (ARPU - CPI) / ARPU

Any marketing campaign should be measured in this way. A typical long-term ROI is 70% at a minimum.

It is essential to measure in real time so that corrections can be made during the campaign. Today, customizable tools exist to measure the performance of each campaign, and within each campaign of each media placement and each visual, in real time. With this information, the marketer may decide to make changes or cut parts of the campaign, and reinvest budget in others. This is confirmed by Gabe Leydon, CEO of MachineZone: "We spend a lot of money in marketing and commercialization. This can go wrong [...]. Sometimes there is a lot of fraud, a lot of dubious activity. You need to be able to change direction quickly. We buy on a large scale and if something goes wrong, we must be able to change it at any time."[2]

---

2 *VentureBeat*, 2016

Eric Benjamin Seufert[3], Marketing Director at Wooga, shows the impact of the retention observed on the first day on a user's lifespan: a group of users with a retention rate of 50% on the first day (50% of users will never open the game after the first day) has a lifespan of 37 days. If the retention rate on the first day decreases to 40% (i.e., 60% of users will never open the application again), the lifespan of these remaining users decreases to 30 days.

50% Day 1: **37 day** total lifetime

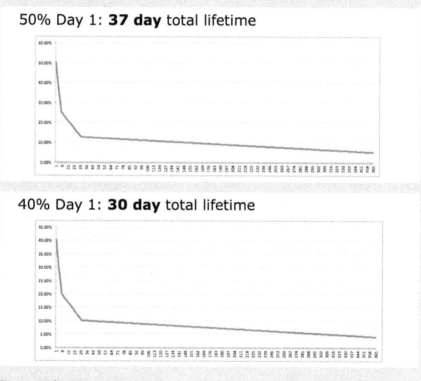

40% Day 1: **30 day** total lifetime

Figure 5.6 – Retention curve

From this curve, one can derive preliminary performance indicators that can be used in optimizing marketing campaigns. For example, the same mobile game might find that users who complete the game tutorial within the first 3 days after the application is installed are generally more engaged in the game and

---

3 Eric Seufert, *Jelly Splash Launch on Slideshare*

have a greater propensity to play it. The marketer will therefore concentrate on the KPI of the percentage of tutorials completed in the first 3 days. Another marketer, in charge of a taxi application, will look at the percentage of users who complete a ride within the first week after the application is installed.

Advertising revenue per use				Purchasing revenue per use	
Length of average use	Number of uses per month	Number of page views	CPM per page	Purchase frequency	Price
3 months ×	15 ×	(5 ×	$5 CPM +	1 % ×	$1.99)
ARPU = $2.02					

Table 5.1 – Simplified ARPU calculation[4]

A well-chosen KPI can be measured quickly after installation, to be able to reorient and optimize the marketing campaigns still in progress. These KPIs can be communicated to all marketing partners, so that they will optimize their media placements as they go along. It is therefore very important to work with an analytical solution that is able to measure these KPIs in real time and to communicate them to the chosen marketing partners.

Let's take the example of an affiliate network. A marketer will be able to communicate the performance objectives of the campaign to her affiliates. By receiving the KPIs in real time, she can then remove or optimize low-performance traffic sources, and grow those with better performance. From this same token, a Facebook marketing agency could identify the combinations of messages, visuals and audiences that generate the best KPIs. This will allow an optimal marketing budget utilization.

WHICH MODEL TO USE?

Performance marketing is an advertising model for which the advertiser of a mobile application only pays after the results of a previously defined action, such as an installation or a sale. Most frequently the model is CPI, but other post-impression cost models such as CPC, CPA, etc. are also used.

---

4 For ideas to develop more complex ARPU models, consult Soomla's blog

The advantage of performance marketing is that it brings results to the advertiser. This proves to be very convincing in the field of mobile marketing. Indeed, it is often difficult to achieve a positive return on investment in a competitive environment where remuneration is based largely on impressions and clicks.

Marketers should take care in characterizing the action to be measured and optimized. A good partner can help you define, evaluate and determine best practices to track the effectiveness of your mobile campaigns, while helping to calculate ROI and the lifespan of users for each campaign.

The 2 most common models of performance marketing are:

• **Cost per installation (CPI)**

Cost-per-installation advertising is designed specifically for the purpose of generating an application installation.

With this model, the marketer only pays for ads that result in an app being downloaded and opened by a user. Through CPI, ROI responsibility is shared with the performance marketing network and their publishers, as they need to ensure that advertisements are appropriately targeted to customers likely to carry out the desired action in order to achieve the performance goals of the advertiser and the monetization goals of the publisher. The CPI model is a great way to launch an application, get a user base and increase its ranking in App Stores.

• **Cost per sale (CPS)**

Cost-per-sale advertising is ideal for companies looking to generate sales through their mobile app. In this model, the advertiser pays for an ad only when it results in a consumer purchase. If there is no sale, the advertiser does not have to pay for the ad. CPS advertising relies on providing purchase incentives to the consumer at a specific time. It can also be used to encourage consumers to go directly to the store, or to e-commerce sites. It uses tracking tools to measure purchase events and metrics.

With no risk for advertisers who the CPS format guarantees an ROI to, this type of payment is generally not very attractive to publishers, who must bear the risk of being paid over time (it can take several days or even weeks between the installation of the application and the first purchase). In this model, publishers also run the risk that the application has a low conversion rate, or that the product does not sell well. To level the playing field, some industries have come up with a hybrid model, for example, a nominal payment on installation (CPI) and a CPS bonus at the time of purchase. This is a typical approach in mobile entertainment (phone ringtones, games, etc.) paid through a phone package.

IN PRACTICE: A REVOLUTION FOR RETAILERS

More and more retailers are choosing campaigns based on performance to stimulate sales through their mobile apps. Travel apps do the same to encourage bookings of flights, hotels and other services.

Since mobile connectivity surpasses that of traditional PC, marketing campaigns can target new customers based on geographic location, device used, operating system, traffic source, and many other features. A retailer can also take advantage of its physical presence to increase the value of its application, for example by providing directions to the nearest store (such as Walgreens pharmacy in the United States), or offering in-store coupons (such as Walmart).

EXAMPLE

Very innovative brands even use mobile as lever for the whole business: Starbucks, for example, sees in its application an extension of the brand, but also a tool for productivity. Inside the application, the loyal consumer will find the music played during his last visit, as well as his loyalty points status. But it will also be possible for him to order his drink in advance, and even to pay at the register with a single click. This comprehensive strategy, combined with smart marketing, enabled Starbucks to increase their monthly mobile active users in the US by 7.5 times between 2013 and 2016[5].

---

5 *App Annie*, Starbucks MAUs, US, Dec 2013 and Dec 2016

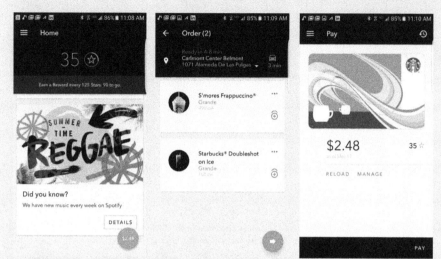

Figure 5.7 – Starbuck's loyalty screen

Figure 5.8 – Starbuck's order screen

Figure 5.9 – Starbucks payment screen

What kind of marketing strategy is needed for this type of application? Imagine that Expedia wants to grow its user base in Canada, France and New Zealand, but only with users on iOS devices. A performance campaign could be put in place to exclusively target this population. In this case, Expedia would only pay for results that meet all their criteria.

With such an array of performance-based campaign options, it's imperative for advertisers to take their time in finding the right partner to develop an effective campaign that meets their needs, particularly, for new campaigns, in terms of volume and geographic targeting.

EXAMPLE

Impact of incentives on LTV: a user acquired from social networks could be more engaged thanks to his friends who would have recommended the application, compared to a user who was incentivized to download the application in exchange for a freebie. The latter will have a lower lifetime and a lower value.

As the lifetime of the user varies according to the chosen promotional channel (social networks, e-mail, news site, blogs), a good partner must offer optimized pricing solutions.

As the lifetime of the user varies according to the chosen promotional channel (social networks, e-mail, news site, blogs), a good partner must offer optimized pricing solutions.

EXAMPLE

Campaign objective: Increase the number of downloads in France.

· Average revenue per new user: $2.
· Campaign budget: $100,000.
· Budget allocated to each traffic source: 20% to news apps, 37.5% to social networks and 42.5% to App Walls.

	Agency A Single pricing strategy	Agency B Modular pricing strategy based on traffic source performance
CPI – news apps	$1	$1
CPI – social networks	$1	$1.50
CPI – app wall	$1	$0.5
Total Number of installs	100,000	130,000
Revenue	$200,000	$260,000
ROI	$100,000	$160,000

Source: MobPartner

Table 5.2 – Impact of hybrid CPI on ROI

The ROI of Agency B is 60% higher than that of Agency A due to its modular pricing scale.

Mobile marketing beyond application developers

We have seen how to create marketing campaigns to promote mobile apps. But the mobile medium can do much more than that. It is also a strategic weapon for brands and mobile websites. App Annie's research perfectly illustrates the mobile marketer's dilemma: should I build an application, or will a mobile site do?

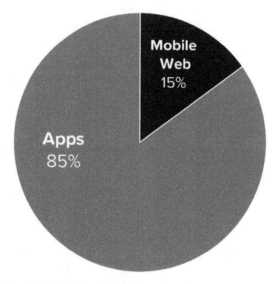

Source: App Annie, worldwide (excl. China), Android, 2016

Figure 5.10 – Time spent in Apps vs mobile web

On the one hand, most brands that already have a digital presence end up with a significant audience immediately transferred to the mobile internet: these users consult the same site from another device. However, this use of the mobile site is very superficial: users spend little time there. Conversely, once the consumer has been convinced to download an application, they will spend nearly 20 times as long in the app. And this engagement is increasing: App Annie demonstrates that time spent in apps has increased 114% across all categories between the first half of 2014 and the first half of 2016, for a total of over 400 b hours spent in apps in the first six months of 2016! But in what circumstances will it be relevant and possible to convince a user to download a branded app?

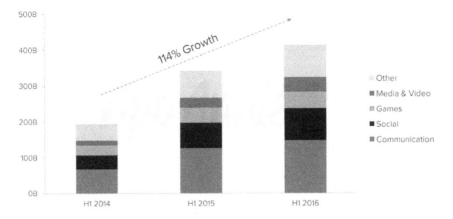

Source: App Annie

Figure 5.11 – Time spent in apps continues increasing

The launch of the App Store generated a tsunami of applications creation. Unfortunately, many have not been proven to provide utility for consumers. In a frenzy of not wanting to be outdone by its competitors, a brand can be tempted to develop its own mobile app. But is that even wise? Once launched, this app will have to be promoted with the hopes of acquiring a critical mass of users and retaining their attention in an increasingly competitive and plethoric mobile world. Indeed, App Annie shows that a typical user only opens between 30 and 40 applications *per month*, depending on their country. That is less than half (and sometimes less than a third) of all apps still installed on that user's phone.

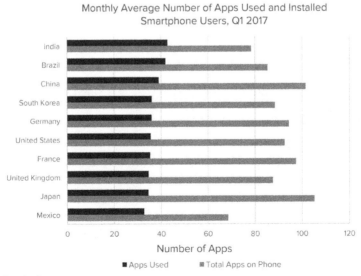

Source: App Annie

Figure 5.12 – Share of apps used compared to apps downloaded

Figure 5.13 – Cartier's iOS application

Many traditional brands that have been built in something other than a mobile-first world cannot reasonably expect to be included. As an example, how many users would install an app about Hershey's products?

Others, such as luxury brands, need to offer engaging and frequently renewed visual experiences, but not necessarily sell their products directly on mobile – rather, they would aim at extending engagement.

Finally, other brands have developed a very strong online business, which can easily adapt to the mobile internet. For example, Expedia, Airbnb or Amazon come to mind.

They must therefore be ready to pursue a dual-track marketing, promoting their mobile site on the one hand and their application on the other – not to mention the fact that they must be able to redirect users intelligently between both of them, depending on whether they have already installed the application or not. This is *deep-linking*, which will be discussed later.

Aim for notoriety, image and engagement: mobile for brands

Always connected, always in symbiosis with the user, the mobile device is a cornucopia for the marketer wanting to establish and strengthen a relationship with consumers.

Mobile is a distribution and communication channel that brands can no longer afford to ignore. In 2016, mobile advertising in the US accounted for over $45 billion (with a drastic rise of 45% compared to the previous year), representing a huge 64% of total digital spend[6].

6 eMarketer, 2016

The mobile medium is extraordinarily effective for brands. As Nielsen demonstrates, a mobile branding campaign delivers a higher performance than a desktop campaign, especially on purchasing propensity measures.[7]

Mobile is the perfect vehicle for allowing brands to conduct virtually individual conversations with their fans and consumers. This is the trend of *"one-to-one"* marketing, where each message is customized for each user, or at least it appears to be. Generation Y, which increasingly controls the purse strings[8], expects that its preferred brands will have a mobile *presence*. The next generation, generation Z, expects favorite brands to be *responsive* on mobile. This generation is almost entirely visual, as evidenced by the success of mobile video platforms such as Snapchat, Instagram, and others. This is great for marketers because video is perfect for brands, allowing them to show their products interactively and engagingly.

From fast food to luxury, many brands have created an account on Instagram, and send their subscribers attractive photos:

Figure 5.14-Burger King on Instagram   **Figure 5.15-Dior on Instagram**

---

7   *Nielsen/Mode Media*, 2016
8   *KPCB Internet Trends Report*, 2016

Figure 5.16-Guerlain on Instagram

Figure 5.17-Photo "liked" by Instagram users

To avoid missing out on the 400 million active monthly users of Instagram[9], brands must create an account, and then be found and chosen (subscribed to) by '*Instagramers*'. Subscribers become an integral part of the marketing campaign, in a logic of co-creation (Roederer and Filser, 2015), sharing, annotating and "liking" the best photos.

Instagram (and others) offer promotional formats to brands. For example, by inserting an advertising video into a conversation between friends (watch out for fails!), or by adding a clickable link to buy the presented products.

---

9   *Statista, Global Social Networks Ranked By Number of Users*, 2014

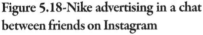

Figure 5.18-Nike advertising in a chat between friends on Instagram

Figure 5.19-Product catalog with clickable links (Clinique on Instagram)

Beyond traditional formats, 2016 marked the commercialization of Chat Bots. In April 2016, at its annual developer conference, Facebook announced the public launch of Chat Bots in its Facebook Messenger application. A Chat Bot is a small, intelligent robot, programmed by a brand, which informs the consumer of the status of his order, answers questions about the product, and promotes products. Chat Bots are introduced in a limited way and based on user permissions, but they represent a unique opportunity for marketers to cut through the App Stores' walled gardens. Indeed, unlike on the open Internet, it is still difficult today to jump from one application to another. Deep linking is still not widespread, and most applications do not lend themselves well to navigating to another application. However, Facebook's *"chat heads"* are persistently on top of any application, even more visible than a push notification. This is an extremely powerful distribution channel for a marketer.

Theoretically, Chat Bots rely on artificial intelligence, which allows the program to have conversations in natural language with consumers, in an automated way (using NLP or Natural Language Processing). Chat Bots have long existed as demonstration interfaces for artificial intelligence software. Their application to mobile is recent, and propelled by the ease of Generation Y to communicate by messaging. The introduction of Chat Bots in Facebook Messenger represents Facebook's response to the commercial platform developed by WeChat (see below). And stems from a very strong desire from messaging platforms to get rid of the Google/Apple duopoly and become the new home screen for mobile users.

In its simplest application, brands can use a Chat Bot to replace customer care messages sent by email or SMS, such as order tracking, delivery estimates, or information about a delay in your flight schedule. A more complex but very powerful application is for a brand to develop a question and answer wizard on its own products or services. The holy grail of Chat Bots is to be able to process natural language inquiries and conduct a 'normal' conversation with a customer. This ideal state of affairs has been portrayed in keynotes about the Chat Bot program, but is far from the reality that the hundreds of thousands of bots deliver on Facebook today. Thus, over the course of 2016, Chat Bots have experienced a roller coaster of popularity, starting from a surge in the summer all the way down to a lot of disappointment in the winter. But Facebook is not giving up, and has publicly renewed its commitment to the fledging medium – and many other messaging platforms have followed suit, such as Viber.

This privileged communication channel can also be used to send advertising messages to re-engage its users, inform them of a promotion, and retain them. Most of the messages will be automated, but until deep artificial intelligence (think IBM Watson-level) can be implemented, human intervention is recommended as much as possible to ensure personalized and sensible experiences.

A word of warning re: Chat Bots: Watch out for abuse! Perhaps even more than other messaging channels, this one is intrusive, because the cthat head will pop over whatever activity the mobile user is into. Chat Bots, in theory, are permission-based, but the feeling of intrusion remains an inherent risk. Moreover, while NLP and artificial intelligence are progressing, the marketer better be thinking through any potential mishap. For example, the Pizza Hut robot will have to correctly decipher the message "I'd kill for a pizza" so as not to cause panic with a call for help from law enforcement.

THOUGHTS ON ZULILY'S USE OF CHAT BOTS

I am a fan of the ready-to-wear flash sales brand Zulily. When Zulily offered to notify me of the status of my orders on Facebook Messenger, I accepted with joy. It was convenient to receive an alert when my order was going to be delivered. It was also convenient to be notified of out-of-stock products. On the other hand, when Zulily began to fill my Facebook Messenger box with advertisements for sports equipment brands, I was less impressed. Intrusive advertising, but not only... given that I do not exercise, and have never bought sporting goods in my last three years buying from you, it was a total let down. If I let you in my private communication channels, I expect that you'll know me a little better.

Mobile: the missing link between the physical and digital worlds?

For more than a hundred years, marketers have faced the same problem illustrated by John Wanamaker's famous quote: "Half of the money I spend on advertising is wasted, the trouble is, I don't know which half." The advent of mobile telephony finally promises to put an end to this dilemma. As we will see in this section, the mobile phone, always present alongside the consumer, can act as a media of the last foot, allowing brands to close the loop between digital marketing activities and in-store purchases. Forrester predicts that in 2016, nearly $700 billion worth of in-store purchases in the United States will be influenced by mobile (compared to the $30 billion spent directly from mobile[10]).

At the same time, showrooming has been the plague of many a retailer, and has caused a decline in sales at physical stores: armed with their mobile phones, consumers went to see a product in the store, touched it, even asked advice from the salespeople, then compared the prices on e-retailers (Amazon, among others), and ended up buying online. The physical store had simply become a showroom, and didn't generate enough sales to cover its high structural costs. Faced with this phenomenon, retailers had to adapt or die (many, unfortunate-

---

10 Forrester, US Online Retail Forecast, 2012-2016

ly, ended up in the latter category, as 2016 and 2017 store closure numbers attest). Innovative retailers survive by integrating mobile marketing strategies in the customer physical experience.

Mobile marketing helps push consumers to buy in-store during one of three phases of shopping:

PRE-PURCHASE: "DRIVE-TO-STORE"

80% of mobile users use their phone to do product research - a huge opportunity for the marketer to present his products and offers, and drive consumers to visit a retail location. Indeed, 60% of these searches end up with a visit to the store.

However, when buying does not happen right away on the device, it is difficult for the marketer to attribute a sale in the store to a specific mobile marketing campaign, and to assess whether advertising has been effective. Micro-localization technologies, such as beacons, are emerging and can allow marketers to accurately identify consumers by their device, and track whether the consumer who saw an advert on mobile went to the store and eventually bought something in that shop.

DURING THE PURCHASE PHASE: PROXIMITY MARKETING

Mobile allows brands to engage in a conversation with the consumer at the time of purchase. It's a bit like placing a salesperson in the consumer's pocket. The sky is the limit to how creative a marketer can get, though generally marketing approaches fall into three main categories:

• **Attracting the buyer:** Proximity technology helps identify potential customers as they approach the store, and attract them through promotional messages. For example, Starbucks will be able to send a push notification early in the afternoon to consumers who are walking close to their stores and attract them with a corresponding promotional offer ("$2 discount on iced coffees").

• **Educating the consumer:** Indecisive consumers in the aisle can open the brand's application and obtain more information about the products without having to seek help from a sales person – and even access deeper knowledge than most sales people would possess. For example, Apple recognizes the shelf in front of which the consumer is standing and automatically populates on their phone information about the product they're looking at.

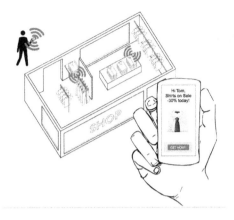

Source: MobPartner

Figure 5.20 Beacons used for proximity marketing

- **Winning the sale:** The consumer entering the pasta department will receive a coupon from Barilla which will convince her to choose this brand.

AFTER THE PURCHASE: RETARGETING

Let's say a consumer visits Banana Republic, looks at white shirts, grabs one but is discouraged by the length of the line for the dressing rooms. A few hours later, this consumer, while playing *Candy Crush,* may see an advertisement to buy the same shirt online, or a coupon to visit a competing brand!

EXAMPLE

Les Mills, a New Zealand athlete, created a franchise of fitness classes that are found in many fitness studios, including Club Med Gym (the fitness arm of the travel giant, Club Med) in Paris, France. Club Med Gym wanted to grow their subscriber base, and use the attractiveness of the Les Mills brand to relate with fitness aficionados. The Mobile Affiliate Network MobPartner therefore placed a promotional offer for Club Med Gym within the Les Mills application. Through MobPartner, geo-fenced users were encouraged to install the application Les Mills, in which they would find a coupon for a 50% discount on the first month of subscription to one of the 20 Club Med Gyms in Paris. The user was then tracked in the gym using MobRetail technology, based on beacons. In one month, Club Med Gym reached 30,000 fitness fans based in Paris and generated more than 600 new subscriptions.

Source: MobPartner

< **FOCUS** >

WHICH TECHNOLOGY?

Four major technologies are available today for proximity marketing, each with their pros and cons:

· **Wi-Fi:** Obtains the IP address of the user. Then third-party services map the IPs to geographical areas.

> Pros: Widest coverage (the vast majority of users keep Wi-Fi connected all the time); no action required by the user; respect for privacy; widespread cartography; availability.

> Cons: Significant error rate (for example, all users using the same network in the same geographical area may be amalgamated); limited accuracy: city level for network-provided Wi-Fi; aisle level in the case of store-provided Wi-Fi.

· **GPS:** Uses the phone's GPS to send the latitudinal and longitudinal coordinates of the user.

> Pros: Good precision (approximately to 3 feet) which allows for neighborhood localization, but also for localization inside a building; widespread use: many applications get permission to geotag their users (for example Google Maps, but also Facebook) and a significant number of users leave the GPS turned on very often.

> Cons: Requires having obtained permission from the user to collect his position data (if your application doesn't have permission, or you don't have an application, you must partner with an allowed application); network coverage issues inside buildings; difficulty to differentiate from one floor to another.

· **Bluetooth BLE:** Beacons are placed at strategic intervals in the store, and communicate with mobile phones using Bluetooth technology.

> Pros: Extreme precision (to the nearest inch): you can follow the user in the various aisles of a shop, and you can even calculate proximity to a specific shelf;

pure tracking use cases require no interaction with the user; battery consumption was greatly reduced by the introduction of the BLE standard.

Cons: Low coverage, as many user turn Bluetooth off to preserve battery life; requires installation and maintenance of a very large number of beacons in store for reasonable utility, to the tune of hundreds of thousands of beacons to cover one supermarket (in addition to the cost of purchase and installation, complexity and maintenance costs - the batteries must be changed every 2-3 years – are almost prohibitive for most retailers); requires user permission, at scale – most retailers don't have a large enough number of users on their apps to start with; very intrusive: the "Big Brother" side of an app that knows exactly where you are can be scary for users - it is to be used sparingly and with a perfectly targeted message to avoid damaging the brand.

- **Audio:** The sound systems of department stores (those that broadcast background music) can be equipped to send sound signals imperceptible to the human ear (ultrasounds), but detectable by the mobile phone.

  Pros: Good accuracy, equivalent to beacon; easy integration into existing systems, provided that these systems are already positioned in the right place.

  Cons: Similar to beacons.

The recommendation is to use the most appropriate and lightest footprint technology. For example, for city-level targeting, Wi-Fi is enough. For neighborhood targeting, it is better to use GPS. At the micro-level, where the utmost precision is required, and technologies bear a higher implementation cost and significant limitations, it is recommended, whenever possible, to combine multiple technologies to maximize coverage and thus, return on investment.

WASTE BINS THAT WATCH US: WATCH OUT FOR "BIG BROTHER"

In 2012, Renew installed very sophisticated garbage bins in central London, equipped with a Wi-Fi system and digital screens displaying advertisements as well as real-time financial and local news, such as subway schedules. During the summer of 2013, these bins were also used to test collecting smartphone data of passersby for advertising purposes. In the span of a week, they recorded more than half a million phones, causing an immediate public outcry, and prompting the city of London to order the immediate cessation of Renew's operations and issue a very public apology.

In the future, micro-location technologies will continue to evolve. Qualcomm, for example, is working on a networked Bluetooth solution in which each mobile phone can become a transmitter beacon. This will help broaden adoption, and once a global standard is adopted, micro-location will be ubiquitous. However, location-based interactions with users will have to remain limited and bring real value in experiential terms in order not to backfire. The trend in micro-location seems to be towards a dual track:

In the first, these technologies are exclusively used for data collection with the objective of campaign monitoring and optimization. In a manner completely invisible to the user, data tracking their path through a particular sales department, their interactions with products, and even their visits to competing stores, will be integrated into any future marketing campaign to improve targeting. This data will be used to create more precise, accurate user profiles. It will also be used to measure the effectiveness of campaigns on traditional media (see example), such as in-store traffic generated by messaging campaigns.

In the second track, data collected by shopping malls and stores will be fed into databases sold to suppliers and retailers. For example, Walmart will, in this context, be able to list all consumers who spent time in the soda aisle, and sell this targeting information to Coca-Cola. Soon, these same stores will know who has viewed a specific shelf, what these people looked at, and what they bought. Brands are obviously fond of this type of information, which is extremely difficult for them to obtain directly, on a large scale and in real time. Another example: the shopping mall's data will allow Zappos to immediately target a consumer who has stopped a long time in front of a shoe shop window.

LINKING DIGITAL AND PHYSICAL CAMPAIGNS: THE MIKADO CASE

To introduce its product, *King Choco*, Mikado launched a billboard campaign coupled with a mobile campaign. They then worked with AdMoove, a French agency specializing in geolocation, to measure the impact of the billboard campaign on the click-through rate of the mobile campaign. AdMoove geolocated mobile ads around billboards, and compared the click-through rate to advertisements broadcast far from the billboards. They showed that the click-through rate increased near billboards in urban or peri-urban areas (city centers, shopping centers, etc.). Conversely, the analysis shows that there are areas where the click-through rate is extremely low despite a significant billboard presence. This is particularly the case near high speed roads (highways, freeways, etc.). Based on this analysis, Mikado concluded that billboards coupled with geolocalized mobile marketing works, provided they are limited to pedestrian or public transport areas, where the consumer can browse his phone in a safe way.

The *cross-device* journey

In 2015, the average digital consumer owned 3.64 connected devices[11]. In a multi-screen world, almost half of all purchases involve several digital devices. About a third of the time, the user decides what they'll buy on one device, but actually completes the transaction on another[12].

An example that immediately comes to mind is the mobile user who is interrupted during a shopping session on their cell phone. After this interruption, this user finishes the buying process some time later on another device, for example, a tablet. This cross-device phenomenon can also occur when it is too complex to complete the process on a small screen. Job searches are a typical case: the job seeker appreciates the immediacy of receiving new offers in real

---

11 GlobalWebIndex Q4 2015
12 Criteo, 2015

time on their smartphone but the user interface makes it difficult to complete pages and pages of job applications. The user will prefer saving interesting offers in their account, and re-visiting those opportunities from a computer interface.

Users simply expect to navigate fluidly from one device to another and don't care about the difficulties this behavior represents for marketers. Indeed, unless users are forced to login to their account every time, on all platforms (as in the case of Facebook), how is it possible to recognize a user in a world where cookies do not transfer from the computer to the mobile? How do you attribute the true ROI of a mobile marketing campaign if almost half of its sales are derived from a computer? How do you retarget a user who has abandoned a mobile shopping cart, and re-engage them to finish the buying process a on computer?

Data is the fuel of digital advertising and cookies have long been the vehicle of choice. The digital advertising industry has relied heavily on cookies since they were introduced in the mid-nineties. Advertising networks, RTB marketplaces, advertising platforms and all players in the digital advertising chain continue to rely on cookies to serve the targeted ads that form the cornerstone of their businesses. In the mobile format, the effectiveness of cookies is more than limited. Indeed, cookies on the mobile Web are reset each time users close their browser. The problem with cookies in an application is that they cannot be shared between applications, rendering them almost useless.

This is why two other monitoring methods, probabilistic and deterministic, have emerged to track users from one device to another; these can be more accurate, and therefore potentially more problematic, from a privacy point of view, than cookies.

ALLISON SCHIFF
Senior Editor at AdExchanger

Deterministic matching taps into known user data to make a match, generally an email address used to log into multiple devices. (Think Facebook, Google, Amazon, Twitter, AOL.)

The probabilistic approach draws on a variety of anonymized data signals like IP address, device type, browser type, location and operating system to create likely statistical connections between devices. (Think Drawbridge, the recently acquired Tapad, Crosswise, Adelphic, Adbrain.)

Probabilistic ID vendors will often use what is called a truth set – a core of licensed deterministic data – to train their algorithm over time.

That makes it sound pretty black and white – but it isn't. There is also a growing trend around data companies like Oracle adopting a blended approach in certain cases, using a combination of probabilistic to complement their deterministic matching capabilities in an attempt to reach the scale of players like Facebook and Google.

The deterministic players – mainly Facebook with Atlas and Google, which final-ly came out with its own cross-device solution in June after months of speculation – are often referred to as walled gardens, aka enticing and effective Shangri-La playgrounds of near-perfect cross-device identity matches where marketers can achieve both scale and accuracy with one noteworthy catch: Marketers can't take their insights with them. What happens in a walled garden stays in a walled garden and can't be used to inform campaigns elsewhere.

Although marketers generally find this state of affairs frustrating, it hasn't stopped them from spending with the big guys, as clearly evidenced by Facebook's and Google's respective blockbuster Q4s.

Facebook has demurred that it's all in the name of privacy. Patrick Harris, Facebook's director of global agency development, has said that if he had his druthers he would replace the term "walled garden" with "privacy garden." (It hasn't caught on.)

Privacy issues aside, the industry is dealing with its own issues, namely how to strike the right balance between reach and accuracy.

A device graph – the mapped connections between devices – is only as effective as its ability to find a lot of matches (reach) with a level of statistically relevant precision (accuracy).

For companies that aren't deterministic titans like Facebook or Google with both scale and accuracy, one usually has to suffer in favor of the other. If a marketer wants reach, match accuracy usually goes down. If a marketer wants exactitude, scale goes out the window.

There's an extra nuance there, though. As Tim Abraham, director of data platforms at Adbrain, explained:

"Accuracy is a metric that doesn't necessarily mean what people think it does. In the context of cross-device identification, accuracy is calculated as the number of matches correctly identified, as well as the number of non-matches correctly identified. In other words, it's the number of times a probabilistic prediction was correct, but also includes 'non-match' predictions from the total pool of predictions it made. Marketers don't care very much about the non-match predictions because they want the predictions of correct device matches. But there will actually be many more non-matches than correct matches, so this massively skews the accuracy score, making it look much better than it really is."

In other words, device graphs are getting credit for being accurate about inaccuracies. It's a head-scratcher.

So is the fact that the two primarily probabilistic device graphs on the market have been verified by Nielsen as being insanely accurate. According to Nielsen, Tapad's cross-device connections are 91.2% accurate, while Drawbridge received a 97.3% accuracy score.

To put that into perspective, when AOL worked with comScore on a verification project in 2014, the results came in at 93% accurate – and that's for a deterministic data set.

How, then, were the Tapad and Drawbridge numbers so high? The answer could lie in the subtle difference between accuracy rate and match rate. While the match rate is defined as how many times one is able to correctly connect two or more devices, the accuracy rate includes correctly identified non-matches.

Nielsen compared samples from both the Tapad graph and the Drawbridge graph to data from its own third-party panel as the truth set.

In the test with Nielsen, Drawbridge's accuracy rate was 97.3%, but its match rate was 10.3%. (Tapad didn't publicly release its match rate.)

There is a fair amount of skepticism in the industry around probabilistic methods and whether cross-device recognition and targeting is as advanced as the vendors who sell it claim.

Most cross-device technology providers are also suppliers of advertising space. This poses a real problem of conflict of interest. What confidence can you have in providers who ask you to share proprietary data to feed their algorithm, knowing that they will probably also work with your competitors?

In 1930, the "rule of seven" appeared, which states, on average, a consumer must be exposed to a message seven times before deciding to buy. Marketers who wish to reach the same target through various media - from television to digital to mobile - inevitably are challenged to adapt to the mobility of their target from one medium to another. Though imperfect, the solutions of *cross-device* attribution that we have seen allow the marketer to create a more precise plan and better allocate budget. Knowing that CPM can vary by a factor of ten between television and mobile, these calculations have a big impact on ROI.

< FOCUS >

HOW BRANDS USE FACEBOOK TO FOLLOW THEIR USERS[13]

Facebook enabled KLM to discover that, although 95% of their purchases were made from a computer, 25% were influenced by mobile advertising. This enabled them to allocate their marketing investments more precisely. Another example is Banque Populaire (through its agency ZenithOptimedia, a subsidiary of Publicis), which discovered, thanks to Facebook, that mobile had been the triggering factor for almost 75% of the multi-device conversions on their campaign for SMBs. Due to low traffic on their mobile site, Banque Populaire had considered reducing their mobile marketing investments -- the discovery of the value of this traffic allowed them to reorient this decision.

In the future, tracking must be able to cross the barriers of connected objects and follow a user not only from a mobile phone, to a tablet, to a computer, but also to a wearable device, or smart home object. These challenges loom large in a world where it is already extraordinarily difficult to link data on the same user coming from just two different sources. Some sectors have long grappled with customer data matching challenges: it is still incredibly hard for the retail sector to map shopping receipt information to a user's loyalty card, even when this loyalty card is scanned at the time of purchase. One can only imagine how complex it will be to integrate external data sources from different platforms.

---

13 Facebook Atlas Solutions Success Stories, 2016

ALLISON SCHIFF
Senior Editor at AdExchanger

THE PRIVACY QUESTION (WITH NO CLEAR ANSWER)

The proliferation of devices has made it harder – in fact, near impossible – for consumers to opt out across devices.

Although self-regulatory programs like AdChoices and AppChoices, created by the Digital Advertising Alliance (DAA), aim to help consumers get a handle on where their data is being used, there are obvious limitations.

For one, the opt-out process requires an heroic amount of effort and industriousness on the user's part. Users who want to opt out have to do so on a per-browser, per-device basis – and then diligently maintain their preferences. It's asking a lot.

The industry is just "not there yet" when it comes to universal opt-out, admitted Genie Barton, VP and director of the Council of Better Business Bureaus' Online Interest-Based Advertising Accountability Program.

"I think it's fair to say this area is evolving rapidly and may be ... challenging traditional consumer expectations about their privacy," said Justin Brookman, policy director of the FTC's Office of Technology Research and Investigation, at the workshop.

For research purposes, Brookman and his team ran a mini analysis of the top 20 sites for news, sports, shopping, games and reference (100 sites in all) to see if they could tell when cross-device tracking is happening.

"We spent days trying to get a sense of what's going on," Brookman said. "It's really hard to determine objectively, from the end user point of view, when cross-device tracking is going on ... [And] that raises the question: How much transparency should there be? What do consumers expect? Do they want to be overloaded with information? If cross-device tracking is going on, what should consumers be told and how?"

There's another question to add to the end of Brookman's list: What are the privacy implications of cross-device tracking when the Internet of Things enters the scene? Arguably, anything that gives off a signal is fair game for the device graph, whether it's an Apple Watch or a connected toothbrush.

In November [2016], an article in ProPublica called attention to the fact that smart TV maker Vizio had updated its privacy policy to say it had begun collecting and sharing cross-device user data with advertisers. Users who weren't interested had to proactively opt out.

A few days after that, a piece in Ars Technica decried a practice known as audio beaconing, which takes advantage of inaudible, high-frequency sounds embedded in ads to track user behavior across devices, including TVs, phones and tablets.

Both scenarios call attention to the thorny issue of what notice and choice, aka privacy policies, should look like in a world where anything that can be connected to the Internet will be connected to the Internet.

The cross-device landscape is still either the privacy Wild West or a hotbed of innovation, depending on your perspective. And, privacy policies, rather than the privacy safeguards most consumers believe them to be, are really just legal documents for companies to protect their derrieres in the case of a breach.

(According to research from University of Pennsylvania professor and privacy pundit Joseph Turow, between 55% and 65% of US consumers believe that when a website has a privacy policy it means that site won't share user data with other companies, which is patently untrue.)

Performance

Some areas lend themselves better to performance marketing:

Marketers wishing to generate prospect lists, purchases on their mobile sites, or coupon downloads, have a wealth of possibilities but face specific constraints on mobile.

Many products are still difficult to buy on mobile as they require a conversation with an expert. For example, most insurances are sold after a consultation, so insurance marketing focuses on lead generation, i.e. getting prospects to give out their contact information in a form and agreeing to receive a call from an insurance agent. Mobile is a relevant channel for lead generation, but unfortunately also a fertile ground for fraudsters. Indeed, it is very easy to create a robot that enters fake identities on registration forms. The good news is that the validation tools developed for lead generation are generally effective on mobile. Solutions such as LeadIq or Forensiq are very successful on the market.

Let us now look at m-commerce (shopping from mobile), specifically. m-commerce has long lagged behind e-commerce (digital shopping on the computer) for a couple of reasons: the size of the screen made merchandising difficult, and consumers were reluctant to share their credit card details on mobile. The advent of secure payment methods, as well as the adaptive presentation standards for mobile Internet, including "responsive" dynamic sites, have changed that. In the United States, the period between Black Friday (the day after Thanksgiving) and Cyber Monday (the following Monday), serves as a gauge to measure the shift of commercial activities to digital devices. Predictably, from year to year, m-commerce nibbles away market share, carried in large part by Amazon and eBay. Adobe estimates that over $1 billion was spent in the US on mobile, on Black Friday 2016 alone – representing a 33% year-on-year increase. Europe is witnessing the same shift towards m-commerce, which brought in 65 billion euros in 2016[14]. This global trend is corroborated in Asia by the success of Singles Day in November (11.11), one of the biggest digital trade events in China. This online shopping mass is breaking new records: in 2015, more than $14 billion was spent in one day on the Alibaba platform, representing 60% growth compared to 2014. Even more stunning, almost 70% of these purchases were made on mobile - a phenomenal acceleration compared to an already impressive 43% in 2014.

In the beginning, mobile sites were often shrunken versions of desktop sites. As a result, pictures were badly positioned, the font was tiny, input fields were hard to tap, etc. In short, it seemed everything was done to discourage the consumer from buying.

The advent of responsive design, that self-adapts to the size of the screen, allows brands to build a single site that can be seen from any screen size. It is much cheaper than having to develop dedicated sites for each device used (mobile, tablet, computer).

Once issues of screen ergonomics are resolved, the marketer can launch performance marketing campaigns. The focus on user experience must remain at the heart of marketing think though. For example, it is established that a large part of m-commerce takes place from a tablet. The marketer shall therefore measure

14   RetailMeNot and Centre for Retail Research, 2016

this that proportion for his brand and modify campaign allocation accordingly. Traditional web tools such as Google Analytics are perfectly suited to this task.

Note that the mobile phone is a very good support to distribute coupons, especially for consumer products. As it is carried to the store by the consumer, it replaces paper coupon-clipping. With regard to coupons, avoiding fraud is a central concern. The Quotient Technology (previously known as Coupons. com) subsidiary Shopmium, remedies this and simplifies the redemption process by reimbursing consumers for taking a photo of their receipt.

CASE STUDY

SHOPMIUM

A brand of dairy products wanted to introduce a new type of "super filling" dessert yogurt, lighter in fat.

Their objectives:

· Introduce this new product range.

· Recruit new consumers.

· Collect consumer opinions on tastes and product.

· Survey how competitors are perceived.

The solution:

· Shopmium created a promotional offer with a progressive rebate :40% refunded for 1 yogurt purchased, 60% refunded for 3 yogurts purchased.

· Shopmium promoted this offer to their users, by newsletter, by push notifications, and on social networks, as well as through a contest.

Figure 5.21 – Shopmium promotion for a brand of yogurt through Facebook, newsletter and push notification

The results:

· In 5 weeks, the campaign garnered 4 million impressions, and almost 50,000 consumers purchased a total of more than 130,000 yogurts - over 20 tons of product!

· The campaign reached strategic consumers:

- Who bought more (8 cartons on average during this month, instead of 2 cartons and a half per quarter typically);

- Who discovered or rediscovered the brand (65% of buyers);

- Who discovered the super-filling yogurt category (48% of buyers);

- Who consumed competing brands (89% of buyers);

- Who were loyal: 86% plan to buy the product, 88% would recommend it.

After-sales communication through the mobile app enabled the dairy brand to decipher the preferences of its consumers:

· Two flagship references (vanilla and raspberry are the preferred flavors) and desires for new flavors.

· Two consumption habits (as a dessert or as a snack).

· Nearly 5,000 consumer opinions collected.

The challenges of building loyalty

Mass user acquisition is enormously expensive and time consuming, not to mention the fact that the loss of these new users is rapid. Therefore, the key to the acquisition business is not quantity, but quality. That is, a user that opens the application and uses it as regularly as possible and for as long as possible. Worryingly, statistics stack up against marketers in this regard:

- Only 10% of mobile users still use an application one week after downloading it; this figure drops to 2.3% after one month.[15]
- Even passionate users get tired: half of the applications have lost their best users after three months.[16]
- In addition, it is much easier to sell to existing consumers than to new consumers. Intuitively true, this is also demonstrated by a myriad of statistics[17]. To collect a dollar of revenues, it will cost you five times more with a new user than with an existing user.

Here we will explore the keys to retention, re-engagement and re-targeting of users.

A way to improve retention is to continually make changes to the application. Indeed, one of the choice criteria for an application, is its evolution and its update frequency (see the chapter on ASO). If an application evolves continuously, it sends a very positive message to the target user, because it demonstrates that it takes into account its evolving ecosystem to always create a better offering.

15 TapStream
16 BI Intelligence, 2015
17 Alex Lawrence on Forbes, 5 customer retention tips for entrepreneurs, 2012

Be careful, though: updates inevitably face two major obstacles. The first concerns obtaining the approval of the App Store. Thankfully timelines seem to be shortening (they have gone from about 8 days to 1-2 days), but there is still a risk that your changes are rejected. And publishers have very little recourse in that case. It is always down to the goodwill of the App Store, which can at worst reject the whole update, and at best require modifications. Savvy marketers circumvent the approval process by implementing A/B testing software (which we will review later) to test minor updates to the app. Note: Google Play does *not* have a review process, so any changes can be made available to users immediately.

The second obstacle relates precisely to the engagement of this B2C target. Although updates are now processed automatically for most users (exact statistics are unknown, but since this is a core functionality of the platform that is enabled by default, one can expect large adoption), an update message will remind your users of the presence of your application. If at this point the user no longer finds immediate use for your application, the update may unfortunately be the action that triggers an uninstall. If, in addition, the permissions required by the application change, you will again have to obtain the explicit agreement of users: this creates a moment of reconsideration equivalent to an initial purchase consideration. In all cases, the user must justify for themselves: "Why do I have this application on my phone?". In a world where mobile users, on average, use about 30 applications a month[18], the weight of this question is enormous.

FACT SHEET

SOME IDEAS FOR LOYALTY

The subject of loyalty is vast and idiosyncratic to each application --the magic recipe that makes an app's user hooked or not. Some ideas to explore:

· Establish a strong partnership between the product team and the marketing team to visualize and improve the entire user path, from acquisition, through to product experience and retention. The best ideas require the collaboration of the whole team to be implemented.

· Delight the customer: Identify the moment when users become tired and send them a small gift (a personalized emoticon to use in their messages, a promotion on their favorite products, etc.) just before.

---

18   App Annie, Q1 2017

· Surprise the users and stay in tune with current events: Beyond simple season-al promotions (e.g., HayDay dressing cows in swimsuits at the beginning of sum-mer), look at Uber, which creates localized, ultra-targeted promotions: in London, to celebrate cat day, Uber let stressed City workers rent a kitten through its ap-plication, for petting and cuddling time; in Beijing, Uber gave ambitious entrepre-neurs the chance to share a ride with a renowned CEO; in San Francisco, on the day of the legalization of same-sex marriage, you could order a limousine on Uber, complete with an officiant, and get married on your ride.

Finally, it is necessary to take a global view of loyalty. Consider for example, a publisher with multiple applications, facing a user who gets tired of one of them. If they find out that the user is about to drop out, that publisher can try and direct her to another application in its portfolio (cross-selling), rather than losing her altogether. The Japanese GREE, which has a portfolio of mobile games, identifies users who the data indicates are starting to get tired (decreas-ing frequency of play, lack of progress in the game, shorter sessions, etc.), and fills ad slots in those users' games with ads for other games from their portfolio, instead of external ads.

The keys to re-engagement

The question here is how to reactivate users that had engaged with the applica-tion but no longer are - all those passive users who have not opened the appli-cation recently. To do this, 3 main tactics exist.

The first is the use of push notifications. Through these, the target user is told that it would be good to return to the app. To be effective, that message needs to be personalized by highlighting what's new since the last time the user visit-ed. New features, or new products, should be presented. Why would the user return to play your game? Maybe one of their friends has dethroned them? Mine all available data to create the optimal message and drive win backs.

But beware: users are very sensitive to an excess of notifications. This is even more true for inactive users, to whom marketers must demonstrate another level of relevancy. If the user feels pestered, they will uninstall the application altogether.

The second is re-targeting: The user seems lost... What to do? First, we must learn the lessons of our failure. Software, such as Uninstall.io, will analyze causes and sources of uninstallation. If all is not lost (i.e. perhaps the consumer just didn't have time for us but thought the app was OK), we must try to find this mobile user and convince him/her to come back. For example, if a successful game such as Zynga's *Words with Friends* has a new version, it is possible to aim a marketing campaign to users of the first version, even if they do not open it anymore.

To target exclusively these users, one will need a list of their unique identifiers (GAID on Android and IDFA on iOS). Then, the marketer will try and find these users as they go about their typical mobile browsing habits. She will upload the target user list on DSPs, Facebook and other distribution channels, so the marketing campaign will be exclusively visible to these users (it is it recommended to customize messages and visuals accordingly). We must not forget, however, that this tool will be limited to large-scale cases only – after all, you are trying to solve a 'needle in a haystack' kind of problem. We also need to think about the cost of targeting. Paid CPC, the cost of re-targeting will be added to the initial cost of acquisition (CPI) to calculate the ROI on these users. This leaves a margin of maneuver that is quite low.

The last is a tool of last resort. It is possible to encode a screen that appears when uninstalling an app. It's unlikely to convince a user to stay, but can be effective in gaining feedback as to why they're leaving (to improve your application,) or to suggest another application from your portfolio, e.g. "We are sorry to see you leave. Do you want to try this Solitaire game?".

The essentials

· **KPIs must be defined** to model campaign performance, to calculate the ROI of these campaigns, and to adjust in real time.

· **The calculation of the LTV** is based on 3 main factors: monetization, retention, and virality.

· **A well-chosen KPI** can be measured easily, quickly and in real time. It will be communicated automatically to all marketing partners.

· **The CPI model** is very popular for developers and publishers. Google and Facebook are dictating a CPC model. Finally, CPM is used on the programmatic exchanges.

· **The advantages of developing an application** vary. Brands like Amazon have a direct need (e.g., a distribution channel), but traditional brands may invest primarily for experiential continuity on mobile.

· **Mobile** is an unrivaled opportunity to connect the physical world to the digital world, enabling a finer tracking of marketing campaigns, as well as innovative interactions at the point of purchase. Steer clear of the "big brother" scenario.

· **Tracking users** from one platform to another, from mobile to computer, is a real challenge for the marketer. Cross-device technologies struggle to follow the mobility of users and few players today can recognize a user on a new platform. The challenge continues with the advent of connected objects, which multiply potential platforms, and points of contact.

· **Marketing objectives** are not limited to acquisition, but must include retention, retargeting and re-engagement.

CHAPTER 6
MOBILE MEDIA: TRAFFIC SOURCES

Executive summary

· **Large mobile manufacturers** have developed proprietary audiences and distribution channels by controlling devices or operating systems.

· **Alternative platforms**, such as Facebook and Amazon, generate traffic, each with their specificities, and develop sophisticated technologies to monetize their audience. Likewise, "mobile first" social networks, such as Twitter, Snapchat, or WeChat have become indispensable traffic sources.

· **Individual applications** are also sources of traffic that call for monetization, whether through advertising or premium models.

· The market has been inundated with increasingly elaborate **technology platforms**. The multiplicity of actors, technical complexity, and the constant chase for zero-latency action and reaction create a shifting landscape that requires sharp skills to navigate.

· Last, we will review **App Stores;** most app installations transit through an app store, making the channel a particular, yet indispensable one.

Mobile Media Channels Typology

Today, about 80% of mobile media is consumed via applications, and the remaining 20% via mobile websites[1]. So, what media channels should you use to reach your target? New types of mobile media are being developed everyday: virtual reality, internet of things, etc. Which platforms are well positioned to develop successful advertising formats?

---

1 *Google Think*, 2015

The concentration is blatant: in 2015, the Google and Facebook advertising platforms controlled more than half of total mobile advertising revenues worldwide:

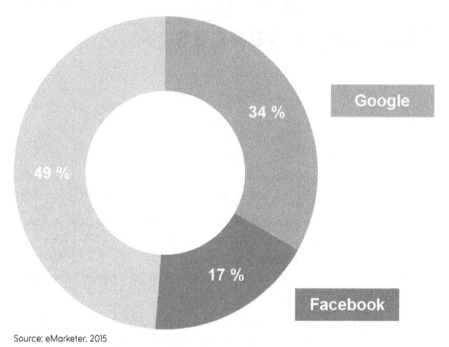

Source: eMarketer, 2015

Figure 6.1 – Google and Facebook Lead Global Mobile Ad Spend

But there are many other actors. Apple is of course one of these, but so are a myriad of DSPs, ad networks, individual apps or app networks, vying to survive and thrive. In this chapter, we will explore the most important types of media, as well as indispensable suppliers.

The App Store

Two-thirds of applications are downloaded via one of the two main App Stores[2]: Apple App Store for iOS, and Google Play Store for Android. Knowing that Apple wants to maintain the impartiality of its results and only allow very limited advertising within the App Store, it is crucial to optimize one's organic app, or content, ranking. This is known as App Store Optimization ("ASO").

---

2 *App Annie, Mobile App Forecast,* 2016

To be highlighted by Apple's editorial team and become a featured App is the holy grail of any marketer. Just a few hours at the top of the list can yield hundreds of thousands, or even millions, of downloads. We will therefore devote a specific section to ASO.

At its annual developers' conference in 2016, Apple announced the introduction of paid advertising inside the App Store. This fundamental change, which brings Apple closer to how Google Play operates, enables wealthy publishers to buy visibility into the most popular application discovery medium. Based on the now defunct iAds program, this marketing channel embodies Apple's desire for control of the user experience and design quality by two specificities[3]:

- Marketers do not control the ad unit. Instead, the ad is created from pre-existing elements of the App listing (title, keywords, description, logo, etc.). Marketers cannot create and upload new ads, images, or copy, which means that if they want to change their ads, they would need to update their actual app name, screenshots, video, or description. This ensures a good user experience, as the ad approval process is essentially the App Store approval process.
- Relevancy matters more than bid price. Ads with poor click-through rates will stop being shown, irrespective of how much a marketer is willing to pay. This also ensures the quality of the ad pool, and has successfully been implemented by other large search platforms, such as Google.

Additionally, Apple now provides a trove of invaluable data to advertisers. That includes the keywords that people searched on before clicking on their ads, which helps app publishers understand their potential users better. This is data that iOS app marketers have never received before, and it's incredibly helpful in determining what potential users the app is attracting. In fact, getting access to this data is probably reason enough to run at least some low-level paid user acquisition campaigns with Apple. The newly available data also includes keyword popularity. This is tremendously important for mobile marketers because it tells them what keywords to focus on when improving App Store optimization. Focusing on keywords that 10 people search for is clearly a bad idea if they can focus on keywords that 10 million people search for.

---

3 App Annie Insights, 2016

So far, Apple is touting extraordinary results: up to 5 times cheaper cost per install than other traffic sources (in December 2016, mobile analytics company Singular told Adweek that the average cost per install for Apple Search Ads was $1.31, while app-install ads on social platforms averaged $5.84, and display ads cost $2.99).

Brands are actively seen participating, whether in an "offense" strategy (bidding on competitors' brand names) or in a "defense" strategy (bidding on one's own brand name); whether to protect one's top ranking (a top app paying to retain user's attention) or to leap-frog the rankings (a new app buying their way to the top).[4]

However, many marketers are left to wonder whether they would not have received these installs for free before: indeed, the new paid ad pushes organic results below the fold (i.e., apps that would appear for free during a search are now harder to see), and the marketers' hand is forced in deciding whether to advertise with Apple Search Ads or not.

Last, by controlling the platform, Apple has access to a tremendous amount of personal data about its users (which it has decided not to use for the moment), and issues targeting standards of its users. To accomplish this, Apple has introduced the IDFA ("ID for Advertising"): a unique identifier that remains anonymous. By using the IDFA, marketers can therefore target (or re-target) specific users without having access to their personal information, such as name and phone number. We will later see how to take advantage of that IDFA.

Google's galaxy

The Google Play store works similarly to the App Store: paid advertising related to search results, and a fierce competition to be selected by the editorial team. The latter will be covered in the ASO section. However, Google's dominance in the app marketing landscape comes from its many distribution channels (Google Play, Search, YouTube, Display Network), representing as many advertising opportunities, and unified under the single banner of Universal App Campaigns. This has enabled Google to drive over 3 billion app installs (ahead of Facebook's 2 billion installs generated worldwide, to date).[5]

---

4 App Annie Insights, 2016
5 Tune, 2016

Whether the marketer chooses to use Universal Ad Campaigns, or to target individual Google channels, app install ads will be shown in Google Play. Ad formats and bidding mechanisms are dictated by the chosen placement. Google quotes Nordeus, a global gaming app developer, as achieving 9X growth and higher user lifetime value and retention through the use of paid marketing on its channels[6].

As a search engine, Google enjoys more than 95% mobile market share in the US and worldwide, except for China and Russia[7] - a true monopoly. The consumer's habit to consult Google for any question also applies to the search for applications: 27% of applications are found after a Google search on all platforms combined[8] (e.g. when a user types "mobile game" or "best calendar application" into the Google search engine). Obviously then, it is vital to be present on the search results page, preferably both in organic and paid results (interestingly, it has been measured that paid results do not cannibalize free clicks, quite the contrary, since a brand present on both placements has a higher click-through rate for each type of placement). This is achieved through SEO (Search Engine Optimization for organic results) and SEM (Search Engine Marketing for paid results), techniques that are well known to digital marketers.

However, mobile creates considerable difficulties for SEO and SEM marketers: the screen size does not allow for more than 2-3 ads to be viewed, with the first ad syphoning off the majority of attention and clicks. Competition is fierce to show in the first place, which leads to high CPCs. In addition, keywords (or key phrases) typed by users are shorter and simpler (more frequently, they will use a quick description like "better calendar app" rather than the longer and more explicit version they would use on desktop, "app that can manage several calendars and connects to Gmail"). This further increases competitiveness because all applications in the same category compete for the same keywords. Note that travel, technology and local information applications receive most mobile searches[9].

Budgets aren't enough to guarantee a top spot. Marketers also need to optimize sites for mobile use: Google has made it very clear that it favors sites adapted to mobile. Whether it refers to the use of "responsive" web design technology, or URL + HTML code, doesn't matter, provided that the page content is redesigned to be quickly downloadable and presented in a readable way to mobile users. Ergonomic criteria are also taken into account to deliver an optimal experience to mobile users.

---

6 *Think with Google*, 2016
7 MarketShare *Hitslink*
8 Google
9 Google

In addition to Search and Google Play, Google offers advertising opportunities on a number of proprietary applications: Waze lends itself to local marketing, YouTube to video advertising, etc. Most of these applications are accessible from a centralized Google campaign. This makes it possible to choose between the different formats and types of media available (search engine, banners on mobile sites and applications, videos, etc.) and to target specific applications, to some extent - some of these proprietary applications are not yet integrated into the system and have to be approached separately for the time being.

As a true multimedia advertising platform, Google has partnered with a myriad of external applications that use their advertising network to monetize. This allows advertisers to target a large portion of the global mobile inventory in one campaign. This platform stems from the integration of AdMob, one of the first mobile advertising networks, which Google bought in 2001 for $750 million, with AdSense, the contextual internet advertising network for mobile or non-mobile, AdMeld, the mobile ad server that Google bought in 2011 for $400 million, and AdX, Google's programmatic ad exchange. Recall, too, the connections to the various Google applications mentioned above, and the power of Google analytical tools (Google Analytics) and marketing tools (such as DoubleClick's ad server).

In addition to their impressive penetration and plethora of offers, Google possesses a competitive strategic advantage by being the operator of the Android platform. This gives it access to user profiles as well as the ability to define access standards for all other advertising platforms. Like Apple, Google has also launched a unique and anonymous advertising identifier, GAID ("Google Advertising ID"), though the comparison ends there. Indeed, because of its digital dominance, Google is able to follow a user on own & operated or partner media, and from device to device, whether they are PC, mobile, iOS or Android. This allows for fine-tuning of marketing campaigns to increase ROI.

The search and navigation model, at the heart of Google's system on PC, is put to the test on mobile. Closed ecosystems do not allow an easy navigation from one application to another and the search conditions in app stores are not ideal for the discovery of new titles. It is quite possible that this system will be completely reinvented, or rendered obsolete, by creating a platform that would siphon off users before they even start a search. This is the holy grail for messaging platforms, such as WeChat, which integrate services directly into its application, or Facebook Messenger, which allows brands to communicate directly with users.

To defend its advantage, Google recently launched the Gboard keyboard, a true Trojan horse. Indeed, under the guise of being an alternative keyboard like so many others, Gboard accesses, with a single keystroke, many Google services, such as the search engine, Google Now smart cards ("It's time to go to your meeting"), Google Maps, etc. The simple interface concedes its true power, because this keyboard is available on any platform, including iOS, and allows short-circuiting of other applications such as Apple Maps, Yelp, or even Giffy.

EXAMPLE

A consumer who types "dancer" on her Gboard keyboard will be presented with a series of emoticons of dancers that she can tap and send in her message. If she types "sleeping cat", she can easily have access to a small animated GIF image. And if she types "restaurant", Google's search engine will propose a list of restaurants located close to her. All this without opening a single app!

In terms of advertising models of the future, Google has a few irons in the fire, courtesy of its parent company Alphabet's foray in the internet of things. The purchase of Nest (connected thermostats) in 2014 for $3.2 billion was quickly followed by the purchase of Dropcam (connected cameras) the same year for $555 million. Additionally, Google announced at its Google I/O developers' conference in 2016 the launch of Google Home, a competitor of Amazon's Alexa, representing not only a consistent interface for all of Google's connected objects' programs, but also a critical foray into mastering the medium of the future for search, voice. During the same conference, Google also introduced Allo, an assistant that support chat bots, and DayDream, its virtual reality offer. In 2016, Google also launched the opportunity to "try" an application before installing it. Known as App Streaming, this feature allows users to tinker with the application from the Play Store without downloading it (important to note that this requires no additional effort on behalf of developers). All of this demonstrates that we are at the dawn of a new industry where everything remains to be defined in terms of media, formats, and advertising models.

It is in fact a multi-year strategy that the company is deploying. Connected objects, predicted to number 8 to 9 per person, have limited value in themselves, but add to the ecosystem in two key ways. The first is the collection and monetization of data through analytics and artificial intelligence, while the second is that they are designed to push contextually relevant content in the same way that Google Play recommends applications. Natural interfaces such as voice will allow interacting with humans in a natural, logical and emotional way - that is to say, in a hyper-engaging way. In summary, Google's IoT ecosystem is already here and has only one goal: selling media.

Pussyfooting Amazon

Amazon, the e-commerce giant and pioneer, was founded in 1994, in Seattle, by Jeff Bezos. Its initial core business was online book sales. After surviving the Internet bubble, which destroyed some the most beautiful dreams brought by the new online model, the company began its diversification. Today, Amazon's wide product range includes CDs, DVDs, software, cooking utensils, jewelry, sporting goods..., 39 categories in total, all of which can be delivered the same day and benefit from Amazon's numerous commerce innovations.

While aiming to be the largest retailers in the world, Amazon has built a distribution empire. And it takes a revenue cut of all items that transit through its distribution channels: whether it is a commerce merchandising fee, or a cloud storage fee (Amazon Web Services powers some of the largest websites in the world), or soon a delivery fee (USPS re-opened on Sundays thanks to Amazon's bankrolling), or finally a content distribution fee through its entertainment ventures – and specifically Kindle App Store, topic of this section.

Amazon leverages its retail DNA for app marketing. It selects promotion days, such as *app of the day*, even if it means imposing its terms on publishers. It makes merchandising and marketing tools re available to publishers to facilitate conversion rates, such as the powerful 1-click payment, or Amazon coins.

The discovery process on Amazon is a study in elegant engineering. As a pioneer in e-commerce, it was unthinkable to ignore this element. Depending on the user's consumption and behavioral patterns, other items will be offered. That is what Amazon does better than anyone else.

While Amazon's app store has made a decent showing (600,000 applications covering 28 categories), its reach is still limited, despite Amazon's 300 M customers.[10] This may change as Amazon aggressively pursues new media channels, such as IoT and voice search (through Alexa): Alexa is now counting 100,000 'apps' (known as skills).[11]

Other App Stores and Search Engines

The problems inherent with the discovery of applications gave rise to a whole range of alternative App Stores. Current ones focused on accessibility and discovery, whereas future ones may focus on specific niches, for example children's applications, or applications for supporters of a certain cause. Until now, most of these attempts have been doomed to failure, apart from a few options that are primarily financed by advertising, or that stemmed from unique market conditions, like China.

The supported OS in the alt store is, of course, Android. Firstly, because it is the only open source OS, and it can be modified according to a specific need, but also because the product base is the largest (2.2 million applications).

As for discovery platforms, Getjar led the way. Founded in 2004 in Lithuania, it raised $42 million in three funding rounds. History taught us that the business models proposed (from white label store up to bidding auction) by this company were either not relevant, or just didn't have enough momentum.

Most of Getjar's users were in countries with low ARPU. Despite boasting about 900,000 applications and 3 million downloads a day, the company was bought for only $5 million, which could be described as symbolic in terms of valuation, by China's Sungy Mobile.

The evolution of this industry has moved towards the creation of marketing platforms: the search engine is financed (and biased?) by advertising for applications. For example, AppBrain, an Android platform developed and operated by AppTornado, a Swiss-Dutch company founded by three of Google's alumni, highlights interesting applications; or Softonic, a Spanish company (founded in 1997, 10 years before the iPhone!) valued in 2013 to 275 million euros, cross-sells applications; and many others with various angles on solving the discovery problem.

10 Statista, 2016
11 Wired, 2017

In a handful of large countries, unique market conditions have led to the emergence of significant alternate app stores.

Yandex is Google's Russian copycat as VKontakte is Facebook's. Yandex is the unoriginal, yet popular, Russian response to American internet services. Yandex owns a 57% market share in Russia and also serves Belarus, Ukraine, Kazakhstan and Turkey. Yandex "only" boasts 100,000 applications. The company's App Store is offered as a white label to all actors in the value chain with a focus on manufacturers and telecom operators wishing to address Russian-speaking markets.

The case of China is very peculiar: despite an extremely attractive market size, for censorship reasons, neither Google nor Facebook have a significant presence. Application discovery is therefore deprived of these two major channels, resulting in the creation of nearly 200 alternative App Stores. Mobogenie is one example. Content is distributed on Android and PC, localized and targeted to major Asian markets, such as India and China. Mobogenie has scaled quickly, claiming 400 million users (67 million in India alone), with estimated monthly traffic of 1.25 billion visitors. The figures are probably overestimated but give an idea as to potential reach for those who wish to implement a mobile marketing campaign in these territories.

Xiaomi Mi App Store and Baidu App Store are two facets of a Chinese sovereign policy in telecoms. Xiaomi is a manufacturer and Baidu is the local search engine. Both monetize their respective traffic with their own App Stores. Xiaomi is a large company in China but it's still just one market. To illustrate this point, Xiaomi recently announced that it has surpassed 50 billion cumulative downloads on its platform, whereas Apple's App Store had 50 billion cumulative downloads by mid 2013, and 137 billion in the summer of 2016 alone.

< FOCUS >

FOCUS TECHNICAL DIFFICULTIES RELATED TO ALTERNATIVE APP STORES

Downloading an application through an alternative App Store is a different process than downloading it from the Google Play store. Indeed, the consumer must either download the APK file (application code), by connecting his phone to his computer ("side-loading"), which requires some tech-savviness. The consumer must also consent to warning messages that are quite scary ("Are you sure you want to download this application, which comes from an unknown source?"), and manually adjust settings to accept downloads outside of the Google Play store. These steps are sufficient to discourage most users, except in China where this process is common. Clearly, this barrier set up by Google has helped it to maintain its dominance. Even Amazon, with the introduction of Amazon Underground and its App Store, had trouble penetrating beyond its installed base.

Facebook, the heir apparent

No marketing campaign is complete without Facebook. 83% of Facebook's traffic worldwide comes from mobile, and Facebook generates more than 80% of its revenue through mobile advertising - $5.6 billion in the last quarter of 2016. Facebook controls 20% of the time spent on mobile[12]. This makes it an inescapable heavyweight of any mobile marketing strategy.

Facebook has notably popularized the mobile application promotion model. Although obstinately silent on the subject, it is estimated that Facebook generates between a quarter and half of its revenue by promoting mobile applications[13]. We owe them three innovations: the first is a native format that inserts ads in the news feed in a non-intrusive way. This format offers a much higher performance and has been adopted by other mobile advertising platforms, such as Twitter and Cheetah Mobile, the latter having obtained click rates 8 to 10 times higher than with conventional banners[14].

---

12 Facebook, 2015, US
13 Re/Code, 2014 & Business Insider, 2014
14 Guerrieri A., Casual Connect Asia 2016

The second innovation is the ability to use demographic and psychographic data from Facebook profiles to target potential users from existing user profiles. For example, if your best users are housewives who love salsa, Facebook target this audience in two ways. First, Facebook can create a segment that includes all housewives who love salsa on their network. Secondly, Facebook may suggest trying to target housewives who love painting, as Facebook's algorithm will have found a strong correlation between these two groups. This is the Audience Extension function. By using this function, Poshmark, the mobile and online marketplace for second-hand clothes sale, found that Facebook generates ROI 3 times higher than other distribution channels, and reduced its user acquisition cost by 30%[15].

Finally, Facebook increases its strength by extending these innovations to other applications via the Facebook Audience Network. A marketer can now, in a single campaign, not only target Facebook application users (Facebook, Messenger, Instagram, etc.), but also independent developers who make their inventory available through Facebook's Audience Network. The ability to use Facebook's rich profile data allows advertisers to have confidence in the quality of their targeting, despite the lack of transparency about the exact inventory.

With the purchase of WhatsApp and Instagram, Facebook hedged against the slowing growth of its flagship application but also gained fertile ground to test new advertising formats.

---

15 Facebook

Figure 6.2 - Poshmark on Instagram

In the case of Instagram, these visual formats are not only attractive to brands, but can also deliver a powerful ROI for user acquisition campaigns. In the Poshmark example, Instagram provided a 37% increase in installations at a 27% lower cost[16].

In the future, Facebook is positioned to be a major player transcending the ecosystem's barriers. On one hand, the adoption of Facebook login by thousands of applications allows Facebook to track users even when they leave Facebook applications, or switch devices by going from mobile phone to PC. At a minimum, this provides a precise attribution of marketing campaign results. We can also imagine using this information to enrich user profiles and create new audience segments on the Facebook network. On the other hand, the introduction of chat bots is a very strong sign that Facebook wants to be able to display advertising messages to the user beyond any platform walled gardens. Indeed, chat bots can be superimposed on any application, even eclipsing ads in that application. As a direct, 1:1 communication channel, chat bots are extremely attractive to brands and present unique advertising opportunities. In that vein, WhatsApp, the (so far) ad-free global leading messaging service owned by Facebook, which surpassed one billion monthly active users in 2016[17], announced this year that it will not charge users for using its application, but will launch communication channels for brands, meaning brands can communicate with their subscribers through WhatsApp messaging[18].

Finally, Facebook has invested significantly in virtual reality ("VR") and augmented reality ("AR") with the purchase of Oculus Rift for $2 billion in 2014. Soon, a large number of mobile games, which represent a significant share of Facebook's advertisers, will migrate to virtual reality. Facebook is well positioned to develop the corresponding advertising formats.

---

16 Facebook
17 *Ibid.*
18 *Ibid.*

Twitter

Twitter has its place in the Hall of Fame of the mobile revolution. Launched in July 2006, it changed our relationship to the world and the sharing of ideas. The tweet (140 characters) has become a standard unit of measurement for digital communication.

Artists, politicians and brands all communicate on this medium with its 330 million monthly active users[19]. 65% of US firms with more than 100 employees communicate via Twitter. 58% of top brands have more than 100,000 follow-ers. 54% of "Tweeps" (a fun nickname for its users) interacted with a brand after seeing it in a Tweet (website visit, Google search, content retweet). Com-panies using Twitter as a customer relationship tool experience a 20% increase in their customer satisfaction index.

Beyond the number of characters, Twitter has become a marketing relationship platform for brands focused on visual content, such as retailers: images gener-ate 20% more clicks, 90% more "likes" and 150% more retweets.

The platform was enriched with a two-stage video format: recorded content (for advertising purposes, such as trailers), and live content (via its Periscope streaming application).

The Twitter platform offers three marketing opportunities:

1. Generation of engagement (through content generation and very precise audience targeting);
2. Improvement of performance (through increased traffic and lead genera-tion); and
3. Measurement of results (using campaign analysis and measurement tools).

In the past few years, Twitter has become a complementary medium to tradi-tional media. Though its advertising formats are still fledgling and have been met with mitigated enthusiasm, in a "multifaceted" perspective that we address in several places throughout this book, Twitter stands out as the best platform for brands that want to engage audiences in real-time.

---

19 Statista, Q1 2017

Snapchat

Snapchat is an ephemeral photo and video content sharing application. Every day, more than 150 million people worldwide use Snapchat, and watch over 10 billion videos, an increase of more than 400% from 2015 to 2016[20]. It is the social network that is indispensable for the young. Indeed, more than 60% of Americans aged 13-34 are Snapchatters[21]. As of the time of this writing, it would take close to 800 years to watch all 2.5 billion Snaps created each day.

They post or watch "Snaps", mainly short (and vertical) videos navigated through by scanning the screen from bottom to top. Snaps disappear after 10 seconds, making this application perfect for unedited and potentially embarrassing content. This makes it a perfect medium for Generation Z. Brands who want to communicate with these users have three paid options:

- **Enhanced videos**: A 10-second video inserted in the news feed, which can be followed, if swept by the user, by a longer video, an article, a call-to-action, etc.
- **Geolocalized filters**: Superimposed on photos and videos taken by users in predetermined locations.
- **Sponsored lenses**: Brands create a filter that modifies selfies, for example by animating the eyebrows, or adding a hat.

Few brands benefit from Snapchat today. Partly, because Snapchat, still focused on product innovation, has a limited sales force. But also because marketers are not well equipped to imagine and create the necessary content for this type of platform. However, the opportunity is worthwhile for innovative brands that target young people because of Snapchat's popularity with Generation Z.

Through the launch of Spectacles, Snapchat has developed a proprietary circular video format, in a bid to out-innovate competitive social networks. In a race where Facebook (via its namesake application, but also Messenger and Instagram) is not ashamed of directly replicating Snapchat's features, it remains to be seen if the medium will thrive or if its flame will get snuffed out by the larger incumbent.

---

20 Bloomberg, 2016
21 Snapchat, 2016

Other social networks

If China is one of your target markets, Facebook will be of little use to you. The main social network in China is WeChat, known in China as Weixin (信信). To reach WeChat's nearly 700 million monthly active users[22], a brand will not only have to go through traditional channels, such as creating a WeChat account, but also through more unexpected channels, such as integrating applications within WeChat.

The first consists of creating an account under your brand's name and recruiting subscribers who will receive your brand's messages (with toned down notifications compared to friends' posts). It is also possible to promote a message to a larger circle of users in exchange for a fee.

The second embodies the trend of messaging applications becoming a single-entry point for all mobile consumer activities. Via the integration of a multitude of applications, WeChat is the only tool a user needs to carry out all his daily tasks: book a taxi, send money, buy a soda, or even book a flight. 31% of WeChat users made online purchases through the application[23]. This trend is observed with most major applications in Asia, whether Line, or KakaoTalk; however none other than WeChat has been able to capitalize on it so successfully.

How did they achieve this? Behind its minimalist ergonomics, WeChat hides an application ecosystem within an application. No need to exit messages anymore, just click a button to immediately execute a function. Commercial transactions are made possible by WeChat's virtual wallet, which has become ubiquitous through a combination of personal and network usage.

In fact, WeChat has capitalized on the Chinese tradition of exchanging red envelopes filled with money with family and friends for New Year ("*hongbao*"), by offering an instant and fun process: users

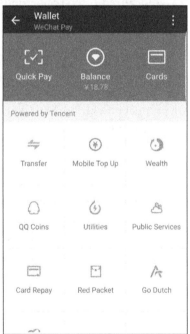

Figure 6.3 – WeChat

---

22 Statista
23 McKinsey, *2016 China Digital Consumer Survey Report*

could send money in virtual red envelopes directly to their contacts' phones, and, by a shake of their phone, had the opportunity to win extra envelopes offered by the application. This virtual money can then be used to pay for services offered on WeChat's platform, using the virtual wallet. This technique enabled WeChat Wallet to quickly gain market share over its competitors. In 2016 more than 8 billion envelopes[24] were sent through WeChat during the Chinese New Year, representing twice the number of transactions that PayPal processed throughout all of 2015, and an 800% growth over the previous year.

But WeChat goes much further than mobile payments. In the example below, the user receives a virtual medical consultation. It is not WeChat that provides physicians, but they natively integrated the medical application Jiuyi160.com.[25]

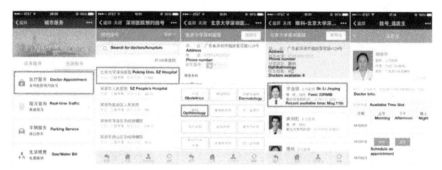

Figure 6.4 – WeChat and Juiyi

Apart from these giants, few social networks reach the same scale and penetration. In a secondary phase of expansion, we can consider Tumblr and Pinterest, but the marketing offering for these platforms is relatively new. The formats vary, although there is a trend towards imitating Facebook's newsfeed approach. Targeting options are limited, as few social networks have a user database as rich as Facebook's, and none have advanced algorithmic capabilities for data mining. The marketer should therefore proceed with caution.

---

24 Tencent
25 Andreessen Horowitz

EXAMPLE

POSHMARK ON PINTEREST

The nature of this application, where young women sell and buy used clothing, is very visual. It therefore lends itself well to the visual search engine that is Pinterest. By implementing Pinterest's Mobile SDK, Poshmark enables users to share photos directly from the app to Pinterest, thereby increasing the visibility of their products and application.[26]

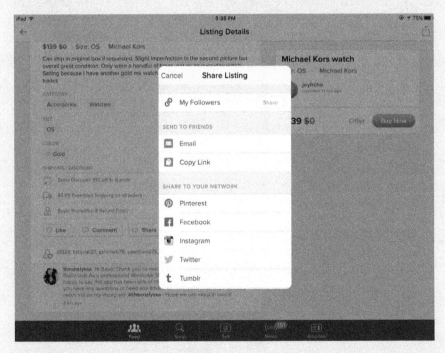

Figure 6.5 - Poshmark Social Shares

---

26 Pinterest

Applications

To get additional reach beyond the above platforms, or to target a specific audience, the marketer can identify individual applications in which to promote their products. For example, a soda brand might like to reach young people on Spotify. Or reach users in Russia on Mail.ru.

Most large applications have developed direct advertising opportunities (in addition to being part of an ad network or a programmatic exchange – see below). They define advertising formats and payment method. Most applications require payment via CPM, but some, particularly utilities, can be paid on CPI. These applications will typically use an external mediation platform and ad server to manage campaigns. After negotiating terms with the application, you will be able to use those tools to launch your campaign.

Apart from the very few applications (around a hundred worldwide), that have either a very large number of users, or an inventory that is specifically attractive to the brand in question, it is not scalable to buy from apps individually. How can we then access the rest of the mobile inventory?

Programmatic advertising

At this stage, the marketer has realized that the purchase of digital media is complex and time consuming. A solution developed in recent years involves purchasing in a programmatic way. Across all media, programmatic buying is expected to account for 50% of global advertising purchases in 2019. In the mobile world, around 28% of advertising purchases were programmatic in 2015, with Magna Global predicting that 50% of will be programmatic in 2019[27]. The resolution of technological roadblocks combined with strong growth in industrialized countries including the United States and Japan will contribute to this tidal wave.

What is it?

Programmatic refers to the automated purchasing of internet or mobile advertising space on ad exchanges in real time, in accordance with the "real time bidding" (RTB) principle. Instead of buying batches of ad impressions, it becomes possible to purchase individual impressions, at a price that depends on the estimated value of each user through an auction.

---

27 Magna Global, 2015

What are the benefits?

The buyer has immediate access to a huge mobile inventory, without having to negotiate a contract, insertion order, or even exactly identify all applications and mobile sites on which he would like to be present. The programmatic purchase allows almost complete automation of the phases of negotiation, purchase, and campaign implementation. On an ad exchange, a campaign can be set up at any moment without there being a direct contact between the seller and the buyer of advertising space.

By applying intelligent targeting and using databases provided by Data Management Platforms (DMPs), the buyer is expected to be able to reach large groups of interested users, and *only* those cohorts, no matter what mobile application they visit. This allows the advertiser to target users with unprecedented accuracy, for which they will happily pay a high price.

How does it work?

RTB auctions: Real-Time Bidding (RTB) functions the same way as the stock exchange. Indeed, each user's impression is put up for sale in real time, in an auction, in which the buyer offering the highest price wins. Practically, this means that in the few thousandths of a second that the mobile site or mobile application page downloads, and before the ad appears, the publisher sends an impression offer, accompanied by relevant information about the user (such as geographical location), in the ad exchange. Advertisers retrieve this impression information, analyze it in real time to estimate its potential value, and decide the price they are willing to pay. They offer this price on the marketplace, where the highest bid wins the auction. The corresponding advertisement is then downloaded and presented to the user, who has no idea of the powerful algorithms making all these calculations behind the curtains, several billion times a day.

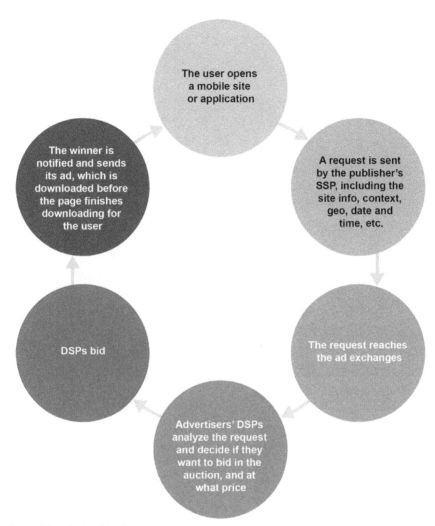

Source: Internet Advertising Bureau.

Figure 6.6 - RTB auctions

The programmatic ecosystem: A comprehensive offer has been developed around the programmatic technology. Ad exchanges are the programmatic marketplaces. Buyers connect through Demand-Side Platforms, DSPs (sometimes via a Trading Desk), and publishers through Supply-Side Platforms, SSPs.

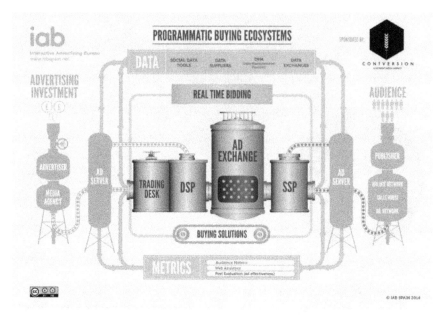

Figure 6.7 - The Programmatic Ecosystem

Here is how programmatic technology automates seven steps of purchasing mobile media:

- **Audience targeting:** In the DSP console, the buyer can choose his targeting criteria: age, gender, interests, etc.;
- **Creation of audience segments:** The buyer creates different campaigns, or content, for each type of audience;
- **Inventory identification:** The buyer can decide to open the campaign to the entire inventory, or target specific ad exchanges, content categories (e.g. all productivity applications), or even mobile sites or specific mobile applications;
- **Purchase orders:** There's no need for a specific purchase order (or IO, for insertion order) for each placement -- with a single contract with a DSP, the buyer gets access to the whole inventory of all ad exchanges the DSP is connected to;
- **Ad serving:** The buyer deals with a single ad server for all placements;
- **Measurements:** The DSP console includes performance reports per campaign, per visual, per placement, etc.; and
- **Optimization:** Reports and data visualization provide real-time feedback to optimize campaigns from the DSP console.

Publishers have the possibility to make their inventory available to buyers in six different ways:

- **Open auction:** The buyer can bid at any time, subject to meeting the minimum price conditions ("floor price") and advertising requirements determined by the publisher (for example, no advertising for alcohol);
- **Invitation-only or private auction (PMP for "Private Market Place "):** As its name indicates, the advertiser must receive the publisher's permission to participate in these auctions. The benefit to both parties is greater transparency and control. Furthermore, the advertiser can continue to benefit from programmatic auctions by choosing specific impressions and offering an optimized price for each;
- **"First Look":** This preferential treatment is a guarantee for the advertiser to win the auction at a preset price if they choose to participate. The advantage is the guarantee of a certain volume of impressions. The disadvantage is the elimination of the process of price optimization created by the auction market;
- **Programmatic Direct (or Guaranteed):** The advertiser and the publisher agree directly on a price, targeting criteria and quantity. This format short-circuits the marketplace and auctions. What is its advantage? In addition to transparency and volume control, this typically allows both parties to benefit from the technological advantages of the DSP and SSP programmatic platforms that they already use (no new insertion orders, no new ad servers). In addition, publishers are generally reluctant to make their best inventory available on the open marketplace, at the risk of not getting the best price. They therefore reserve this inventory for direct transactions. The disadvantage is that it is impossible for the buyer to select only the impressions that interest him: it is a return to the pre-RTB model, only by-passing the manual placement of the purchase order;
- Preferential inventory at a fixed price: **"unreserved fixed rate", "header bidding", "programmatic forward".** Similar to direct programmatic, except that the advertiser can choose, on an impression by impression basis, to buy the inventory or not. In the first case, the price is agreed in advance. In the second case, the price is determined by the auction, with the only constraint being able to participate in the first auctions to obtain the impression (in a waterfall system described in the last chapter of this book). The last case is a hybrid approach between direct programmatic and header bidding that allows for booking an inventory, while keeping an auction system; and
- **Traditional:** Non-programmatic sale, whether direct or indirect, according to the methods previously seen.

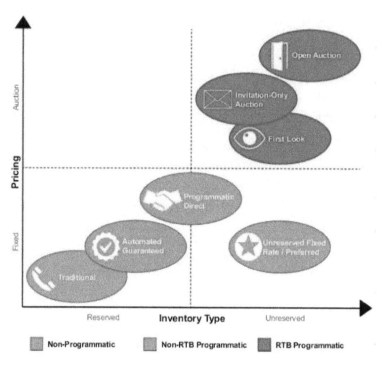

Non-Programmatic   Non-RTB Programmatic   RTB Programmatic

Source: Magna Global

Figure 6.8 - Mobile Advertising Matrix

< FOCUS >

PAYMENTS

In the ad exchange, impressions are sold on a CPM basis. Every player in the value chain needs to get paid: DSPs, SSPs, trading desks, DMPs, mediation layers, ad exchanges, are all paid on a CPM basis, or on a percentage of the final CPM. They are not, however, all paid by the same actors (for example, the DSP is paid by the advertiser, while the SSP is paid by the publisher), and sometimes the cost is simply built in the CPM price (e.g. in the case of an ad exchange).

This has two consequences:

· Intermediation is expensive: The difference between the price paid by the advertiser for an impression and the payment received by the publisher for the same impression can be 30% or more. It is estimated that in 2014, 55% of the sale price of digital programmatic auctions will be distributed to intermediaries, and only 45% to publishers[28]. As the volumes spent on ad exchanges increase, smart players reduce the number of intermediaries (for example, being careful not to pay twice for the same services, which could be provided by a trading desk and a DSP); and

· Targeting is expensive: A marketer must weigh the pros and cons of paying for more precise, but more expensive, targeting with a DMP solution. Using video or dynamic formats also often adds an extra ad serving cost, which must be amortized with a better engagement, or greater user impact.

< FOCUS >

FRAUD

It is widely accepted that the programmatic ecosystem involves significant fraud. A report by Forensiq estimates that one third of programmatic impressions are potentially fraudulent[29]. These impressions may be simulated by robots, or they may result from advertisements that are superimposed on each other, or advertisements that do not appear in the user's visual field. In any case, the advertiser paid for an impression that was not seen by the user.

Facebook quickly concluded from its own experience in the programmatic world that standard formats were so fraught with fraud that they could not deliver a sufficient ROI for its advertisers, who are primarily interested in performance marketing. They decided to focus their programmatic offer on native and video formats, which are less likely to be fraudulent. [30]

What can you do? Paying after the user has initiated an action (for example, paying on a CPC or CPI basis) helps to reduce the problem. If you need to pay on a CPM basis, it is strongly recommended to use an independent verification tool such as Double Verify, Forensiq, Integral Ad Science, or Moat. These tools validate, with the aid of a pixel, whether the impression has been delivered to a user in its entirety.

---

28   Ad Age
29   Venture Beat, 2015
30   Atlas Solutions

The future

The programmatic field is complex, constantly evolving, and rather poorly understood. According to Forrester, 77% of marketers admit they do not understand it much. This is certainly not made easier by the proliferation of players, and overlapping features: DSPs become DMPs, SSPs create ad exchanges, and so on. As a result, the industry is ripe for consolidation and simplification.

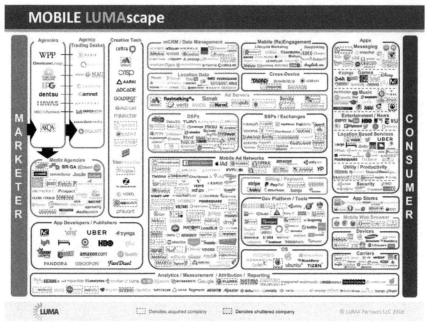

Source: Luma Partners.

Figure 6.9 - Complexity of the AdTech Ecosystem

More than ever, marketers must be analytical and technophile[31]. To fully leverage programmatic buying, they will have to access and master measurement and analysis tools. Alongside consolidation, the market needs to move towards transparency and simplification to ensure it continues scaling.

The rise in competence and sophistication of marketers goes hand in hand with an increase in users' expertise. Users are tired of untimely and poorly targeted advertisements, and the adoption of ad blockers - software that prevents ads from getting downloaded or hides them - has been growing rapidly since their introduction on the mobile market in 2015 (see the dedicated section). It is

---

31 Foundation Capital, *Decade of the CMO*

the responsibility of marketers to care about the user's experience and not just flood them with advertising. This balance is likely to be achieved via a greater adoption of native formats, providing a better user experience and engagement (see section on native formats). However, the majority of the inventory available today on ad exchanges is not based on native formats - rather, the standard IAB format: either full-screen banners, or banners at the top or bottom of the page - and therefore very susceptible to ad blockers.

The rise of ad blockers, coupled with the desire to improve user engagement with mobile formats, will force marketers to continue to innovate programmatic solutions, as they represent the only way for large-scale execution.

Finally, the value of programmatic buying relies heavily on the use of personal data for targeting. Evolving privacy regulation and perception will have a significant impact on programmatic advertising.

Affiliate Networks

A myriad of niche players has been created to compensate for (or, arguably, add to) the complexity of mobile marketing. They aim to connect advertisers and publishers via an independent platform that allows for a one-to-many relationship. Advertisers can discover small publishers, who might host their perfect audience. And publishers can monetize their audience (see Part 3). Generally, these transactions are paid on a CPI or CPA basis to reduce the advertiser's risk. This way, the advertiser exchanges transparency (i.e. does not know exactly where ads are displayed) against performance results, without financial risk. This model is very successful in promoting applications because it delivers scale and provides reasonable pricing. It is therefore very frequently used in addition to Facebook. We will draw up a non-exhaustive but representative list of what the market offers:

Generic networks: More and more often coupled with a programmatic offer, these networks offer worldwide coverage, and (sometimes) direct relations with publishers. Some examples of large networks include:

- **Cheetah Mobile,** the fourth largest publisher in the world, according to App Annie (historically published utility apps, such as CleanMaster and Battery Doctor, and most recently news and social apps)[32], acquired MobPartner to

---

32 *App Annie, 2016*

build a global advertising platform, including its own applications and an affiliate network. MobPartner, originally a French company founded in the early 2000s, rapidly expanded globally until it was bought by Cheetah Mobile, a NYSE-listed Chinese company for $58 million in 2015. The company now boasts having nearly one billion monthly users.

- **Opera MediaWorks** is probably one of the most complete platforms on the market. As the advertising branch of Opera Software, it includes traffic generated by the Opera navigator, Ad-Marvel (a traditional affiliate network acquired in 2010), AdColony (focuses on videos; acquired in 2014), and Moolah Media (an incentive ad network acquired in 2014). Through this single-entry point, a marketer with a large budget can address almost all countries worldwide, on nearly all mobile media. MediaWorks serves 1.2 billion unique mobile devices per month (Source: Thalamus). Opera Software was recently acquired by a Chinese consortium for $1.2 billion.

- **IronSource** (merged with Supersonic Ads in 2015), founded in Israel, dominates the world of affiliate marketing. They claim seeing 550 million devices per month.

- **Glispa:** Founded in Germany, Glispa specializes in mobile affiliate marketing. The company raised over $30 million in funding from electronic and physical commerce giant, Market Tech Holdings, which owns Camden Market in London, to develop its activities in m-commerce.

- **Appnext:** An Israeli company, is one of the only platforms to offer a CPI auction.

- **InMobi:** An Indian company founded in 2007, InMobi boasts one of the largest audience bases with 1.5 billion devices served per month. It has received over $220 million in funding over the years.

Incentivized networks: mainly used in gaming applications, these networks offer a reward to users for watching advertisements. Very popular a few years ago for the huge download volumes they delivered quickly, until the advent of LTV measurements demonstrated the low value of users acquired via this channel. Today, they are used sparingly in so-called "boost" campaigns, for example when looking for a temporary influx of downloads at launch to improve positions in App Stores. Incentivized networks include:

- **Fiksu:** A New England company founded in 2008, can deliver very large volumes (580,000 downloads per second during peak activity). It boasts 38 billion daily impressions.

- **Fyber and Tapjoy:** Two other big players in incentive marketing, they recently diversified (the first through merger, the second through product innovation) to broaden their offering beyond incentivized traffic.

Video networks: by solving technological and monetization challenges specific to the video format, these networks created a niche in the ecosystem. Notable players include: **AdColony** (part of Opera), **Vungle, NativeX** (acquired by Mobvista)**,** and **UnityAds**.

Adult networks:

- **Tapgerine:** originally Ukrainian, relocated to Las Vegas in 2013, it pays 90% commissions to publishers (against 70% as the market's standard) and boasts having over 1,000 campaigns focused on adult, gaming, dating and gambling content.

- **BitterStrawberry**, and **Exoclick** are other examples in this category.

If the marketer does some quick math, they will realize the sum of the audiences claimed by these networks far outnumbers the total number of humans on earth! Very often, networks work with each other, buying and selling traffic and campaigns, making it virtually impossible for the marketer to obtain clear visibility on where their ads will be syndicated. We'll discuss some tips to protect against this later.

Messages

Mobile messages can take a variety of forms: SMS, MMS, push notifications and mobile wallets (Apple Wallet & Android Pay).

< **FOCUS** >

4 TYPES OF MOBILE MESSAGES

SMS

<u>Definition</u>: Text message sent or received by the consumer's mobile phone. It can contain links.

<u>Prerequisites</u>: Requires explicit permission from the consumer for any registration on a list, for example, by sending an SMS with "OK".

<u>Audience</u>: SMS has the largest audience because it works on all types of mobile phones, even the oldest.

<u>Other considerations</u>:
· Limit of 160 characters.
· Ideal for urgent, fast-disappearing messages.
· Suitable for creating traffic at a point of sale.

MMS

<u>Definition</u>: A message sent or received by the consumer's mobile phone that contains visuals, audio and/or video.

<u>Prerequisites</u>: Requires explicit permission from the consumer for any registration on a list, for example, by sending an SMS with "OK".

<u>Audience</u>: It also has the largest audience because all MMS are retroactively compatible with SMS. Hence, any phone that can receive an SMS can receive an MMS.

<u>Other considerations</u>:
· Variable limit up to about 1 MB.
· Some phones can block commercial MMS.
· Ideal for rich media ads, which provide a conversion rate 30 to 50% higher than SMS.

Push Notification

<u>Definition</u>: Content delivered directly from an application that can contain text, visuals, audio and video.

<u>Prerequisites</u>: The consumer must have downloaded the application and activated push notifications.

<u>Audience</u>: Varies by app.

<u>Other considerations</u>:
· Limit of 256 characters on iOS, 80 for display on lock screen; unlimited on Android, but short messages are better anyway.
· Suitable for re-engagement, to push users to reopen the application, via promotional or informative messages.

Mobile Wallet

<u>Definition</u>: content delivered directly inside the Apple or Google mobile wallet. It contains text only.

<u>Prerequisites</u>: The user must actively save each promotional message in his electronic wallet.

<u>Audience</u>: Almost all Smartphone users - Apple Wallet is pre-installed on iPhones, Android Pay on Android phones.

<u>Other considerations</u>:
· Limit of 88 characters for a message saved in the wallet, 33 characters for geo-localized reminder messages.
· Ideal for time-limited promotions, or those limited to a geographical area.
· Can be dynamically updated once saved.
· Very interesting for boarding passes, etc.

Over 560 billion SMS messages are sent each month worldwide[33]. The most common commercial uses include promotions and customer loyalty. Indeed, 55% of users subscribed to a brand to receive promotions, and 52% to receive loyalty points[34]. Messaging is by nature very transactional, and many users prefer that brands communicate order updates (for example, a delivery notice) via messaging rather than e-mail or another mean. Marketers will have good results with this communication channel when used to announce discounts or a product launch, share a follow-up, or even initiate a conversation with the consumer.

---

33 Text Request, 2016
34 Vibes, *2016 Mobile Messaging Guide*

THE MOBILE NATIVE'S GUIDE TO MARKETING

The message may include a link, which is usually shortened beforehand, and must always redirect to a mobile optimized website. An MMS message can also include a coupon for the mobile wallet, an invitation to put in one's calendar, a map to find one's way, a video, etc.

It is essential to pay close attention to both the sending frequency and time of delivery in order to limit the consumer's perception of intrusion.

Push notifications look a bit like text Version 2.0. Not only can they include text, video, audio, links, etc., but they can also take many forms and appear at different places on the phone and at different times. The most common push is a notification at the top of the active screen. But you can also find these notifications on the lock screen, in the notification center, or in the upper right corner of the application's icon. In addition, notifications can include links to specific pages of the application ("deep linking"), or display rich images or content inside the notification itself. It is estimated that about half of users accept receiving push notifications (less than the percentage of users who agree to share geographic location), and approximately half of those will click on a push notification[35]. For all these reasons, push notifications constitute a privileged and very effective communication channel for the marketer.

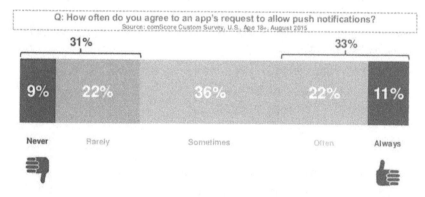

Figure 6.10 - Push notification authorization frequency

Most push notifications have an immediate commercial gotal.

---

35 Localytics, October 2015

EXAMPLE

Poshmark has achieved very interesting results by sending, twice a day, an inspirational and positive message in a push notification. This was a real success in terms of customer satisfaction: users reposted the message on social networks (hello, word-of-mouth) and developed an unfailing loyalty to the brand. Using these types of push notifications Poshmark measured a CTR increase of 35%, as well as an increase in shares on social networks. They also managed to create a unique brand identity for Generation Y[36].

Figure 6.11 – Poshmark's word-of-mouth on Twitter

36   Deziel M., *Inc.com*

160

FACTSHEET

WATCH OUT FOR OVERUSE!

The abuse of notifications will lead to a bad reaction from the mobile user with a range of consequences for the marketer:

- The user disables *all* push notifications coming from your application, and this communication channel is completely lost.

  Tip: Consider using a subtler sending frequency within the application. The user should be allowed to deactivate promotional notifications, but must be offered the possibility of keeping customer service notifications.

- The user installs an app to reduce push notifications, like CleanMaster. After a certain number of push notifications are received (across all applications), this app will send a message to the user (ironically, a push notification!) and offer that they unsubscribe from the worst offenders. However, often the user does not know which app sends which notification, and yours might be caught in the cross fire: for example, Delta might send a promo message, and Expedia might send another one around the same time – if the Delta brand is in both, the consumer might think Delta is spamming them.

  Tip: Demand transparency from your marketing partners in order to coordinate communications and avoid overuse.

- The user uninstalls the application. "Game Over".

The mobile wallet, an up and coming channel, presents very intriguing opportunities to marketers, such as allowing the user to save personalized and geolocalized content. For example, a merchant can send a coupon to his consumers, who can then save them in their wallets. When the consumer is in the vicinity of the store, the merchant can send a push notification to remind the consumer to use the coupon.

MESSAGING

· Consider segmenting your user base so that each group can receive a more personalized message. Even better if the personalization includes a reference to the user's personal or behavioral context;

· Create unique content dedicated to each segment;

· Define a global communication strategy for each specific objective: information, customer service, promotion, engagement;

· Use appropriate language, including short sentences and common abbreviations.

· Vary formats; For example, alternate two SMSs and an MMS;

· Use private messages to send personal information; For example, it would be better to send a boarding pass by direct message (within the wallet) rather than displaying it on the lock screen; and

· Don't forget mentioning unsubscribe options (when necessary).

A myriad of tools exists for creating, sending, and tracking push notifications and messages. Some are combined with application optimization tools. There also are plenty of APIs to build one's own system. The marketer will have to define their needs and compare market offerings. Among the most prominent solutions to consider are Urban Airship, Localytics, Vibes and Twilio.

Partnerships

Partnerships often do not directly report into the marketer, but their influence on growth should not be underestimated. The most obvious ones are partnerships with mobile phone manufacturers, or mobile operators. The publisher may negotiate for a fixed fee, or against future revenue sharing, to pre-install an application on the mobile phones sold by that operator or manufacturer. This is impossible in Apple's galaxy, but remains a very popular option for Android and other OS.

A publisher who manages to sign a partnership with a major manufacturer, such as Samsung or HTC, can expect millions of downloads worldwide. However, many of these will be "phantom users", meaning that they will not ever use this application that they did not ask for, unless it is a brand-name, category-leading app, such as Uber for utility, Yahoo for news, or Firefox for mobile browsing.

Outside of these exceptions, the distribution channel might still make sense, as long as the marketer reduces the CPI to reflect the lack of engagement of potential users.

There is another enticing partnership opportunity: integrating one application into another. For example, an airline application may offer its passengers to order an Uber pickup at destination. Seamlessness and relevancy increase the user's loyalty to each of the two participating applications. This type of integration is still in its infancy, for pragmatic reasons (scenarios that make this useful to the consumer are relatively rare) and for technological reasons, related to deep linking, as we shall see.

Media of the past and future

Is it possible to get a user to download an application outside a mobile medium? Yes.

Both major App Stores are seamlessly integrated on the computer and phone, i.e. a user can send an application to their phone after purchasing it from their computer. Beware when planning on leveraging this though: very often the lag between download and use (for example, the consumer opening their phone again) is significant enough that the user forgot they downloaded the app in the first place!

In the physical world, QR codes printed on magazines, products, or bus shelters, have not really gained popularity outside of Asia or isolated cases in Western Europe. It's unfortunate as they represent a very elegant way to get users to download apps without having to remember and type a name or URL. Technical issues have plagued QR code readers (lack of compatibility, unreliability, lack of standardization). Mega-popular apps like WeChat have defeated these problems by integrating a universal barcode reader and setting a standard.

Television commercials are surprisingly popular for large publishers (MachineZone, Supercell and King spent about $200 million on TV commercials in 2015[37]). A large part of the MachineZone budget has been allocated to the Superbowl, the annual mecca for sports and advertising in the United States. By using Hollywood celebrities such as Kate Upton, Arnold Schwarzenegger or Mariah Carey, MachineZone has created memorable TV spots[38]. But why spend so much money, in creating and buying premium advertising spots? One imagines that the corresponding CPI would be staggering. The short answer is that, beyond generating downloads, investing in a television presence reassures the user and builds trust towards the brand. This, in turn, increases click-through rates (users tend to click more frequently on a known brand or a celebrity), download rates (users are more willing to download a game that they have heard about for a long time), and purchasing rates within the application (one is more willing to give his money to a known application). Therefore, television, in some ways a medium of the past, is still very effective in the mobile world.

In the future, we can imagine that AR will provide even more enticing advertising opportunities. You won't need to imagine how a new couch will look in your living room, you'll just open Wayfair and get a realistic video that shows you exactly what it'll look like. Likewise, Houzz will update a picture of your living room with that couch. You'll design new shelves in the Tylko app directly from your phone, update their configuration based on an AR rendering, and send the plans directly to their plant in Warsaw for manufacturing.

App Store Optimization - ASO

App Stores are at the heart of mobile marketing: almost half of applications are discovered in the App Store:

51%	My friends/family are using them
48%	By browsing app stores
34%	Recommended to me in the app store
33%	Saw an ad while using another app
32%	I read about them online
32%	I see them shared on social networks
31%	Saw an ad while browsing the web
26%	Saw an ad on TV
21%	Through search engines
20%	Saw an ad on YouTube

Source: Google, 2016

Figure 6.12 - Mobile application discovery method in % of users

---

37 Pocketgamer
38 Venture Beat, 2015

It is therefore essential to optimize both presence and ranking in the main App Stores. This section is dedicated to the most important tactics.

Your page in the App Store = the driver of conversion rate

Almost any download goes through the App Store, so the description page of your application is the ultimate portal to convince the user to download it. A huge part of the performance of any marketing campaign is driven by it, so it's necessary to inform, to attract and to convince users in just a few lines and with some images.

To do this, marketers faces many challenges. First, there are format constraints: reduced space, imposed and uniform format between applications (text followed by images and videos, then user reviews). And there is no possibility of personalization, i.e. whomever the user is, they will see the same page.

Here are the main components:

- Title (75 characters maximum for Apple - 54 visible, 30 for Google)
- Description
- Call-to-action
- Screenshots (maximum of 5 for Apple, 8 for Android)
- Demo video (15 to 30 seconds for Apple, 30 seconds to 2 minutes for Google - to be saved under YouTube)
- Categories (for Apple, a choice of 2 or 3, for Google, only one)
- Reviews, stars and + 1s
- Keyword list (Apple only)

For the purposes of ASO, you must carefully choose the title (used by Google as a keyword, see below) and the categories in which you want to appear. For example, an educational game for children could be categorized either under "game," or "education." The first category is much more competitive, but much more popular. The second is less trafficked but easier to penetrate.

The description should be thought of as a marketing spiel. The first 3 to 5 lines must be strong and quickly attract the user: focus on them. Also, quickly display the application's features and highlight recent improvements. If press releases or enthusiastic testimonials have been received, this is the place to highlight them. Don't forget the call-to-action (*Play now!*, *Download and win*, etc.).

Once the user is convinced to continue reading, go into details. Note that much more content will be visible on a tablet or a computer - use this to your advantage.

Screenshots should not be viewed simply as screenshots, but as a story board to visually show case a user's path in your application. It is therefore necessary to choose features and screens representative of your application; do not hesitate to annotate and simplify them for a better understanding. Together, these visuals must tell a story. It is highly recommended to remove any ads from your screenshots!

A video presentation, at the onset, is a phenomenal tool to help the marketer tell a story. What's more effective than showing an application in action? The video must be of good quality, lightweight, short and clear. Think about creating videos that can be understood without sound. And do not forget to translate your videos for each market. Finally, end the video with a call-to-action.

BEYOND THE PRODUCT SHEET

In addition to the app page, the marketer will be able to use other elements to stand out from the competition. Among the most important ones are the application's name, title and logo.

The application's name is crucial. It must be short and descriptive, in a word or two maximum. It is not easy! The name Uber, short, unique and ambitious, is now widely associated with many on demand services: many companies define themselves as "the Uber of xyz". However, this recognition was gained after much marketing investment.

If the budget for building brand recognition is modest, avoid made-up words. For example, the name "Magic Puzzle" is both descriptive (one expects a puzzle) and interesting (what is magic about it?). On the other hand, a name like Kewlio will have a hard time standing up for something on a small promotion budget. Note that Apple only takes the first 55 characters into account in its algorithm. The first few words must descriptive.

The logo is the most important element of all. Indeed, it is the one that represents your application on most screens: in top charts, in search engine results, and also on your users' screens. Your logo must, day after day, convince users to open your application again. It must be extremely clear and visible on the smallest screens. It must be distinctive and representative of the application. A Herculean challenge! Favor bright and clear colors Avoid whole words, but the first letter of the application's name is acceptable. A thorough competitive study should be conducted to ensure that the logo is distinctive from those of similar applications, as well as from those of applications with the same first letter or similar names, even if their goals differ: avoid being mistaken for another!

EXAMPLE

THE DILEMMA OF A BRAND THAT DIVERSIFIES

One morning I opened my Smartphone and my Uber application had disappeared, or, in any case, the white U on the familiar black background wasn't on my screen. That U that catches my eye when I need to go somewhere, or order a lunch. That U that means service, facility and modernity for me, had disappeared. What happened?

Uber was originally launched as an alternate taxi service. As they got more successful, they added many other services, not only around transportation (including carpooling, and even motorbike taxis), but also around other transport related services – it is now possible to have a meal delivered by Uber. Today, the brand is present in many cities worldwide, each with its unique needs and cultures. Tomorrow, they will add driverless cars and many other services. The management team wanted to reflect this development by launching a new logo and a new brand identity.[39]

This new logo - an open circle that surrounds a small square - varies from one country to another, and varies between consumers and drivers. It was a shock for consumers, who generally don't embrace identity change in their favored brands (think: Coca-Cola, or Starbucks).

Uber was fortunate enough to use its market dominant position to force mobile users to accept the change. As the brand faces new headwinds, that may be a luxury they won't have in the future.

---

39 Wired, 2016

OPTIMIZATION AND TESTING

All marketers eventually face an opacity unique to App Store ecosystems: while search keywords are (to some extent) being shared, it is impossible to attribute a precise source location to organic downloads. Indeed, neither Google nor Apple share this information. It is also impossible to create customized app pages per campaign, or per audience. So, it's imperative to maximize the impact of this page for the average user.

Ranking in search engine results

Google Play and the App Store reference more than two million applications each. This is done through proprietary algorithms, the exact formula of which is kept secret so that no publisher can find a weakness and take advantage of the system. Each platform has developed an algorithm reflective of its image: Google, king of the search engines, uses very advanced semantics. For Apple, king of minimalism, a focus on key phrases is used. These respective algorithms are based on roughly the same ingredients, although the recipe differs:

User reviews:
• Average number of stars
• Number of reviews

Popularity:
• Volume of downloads and installations
• Retention rate
• Rate of engagement and frequency of use
• Clicks rate on the application page

Freshness:
• Weighted towards recency
• Recency of the last update
• Time since the first launch

Relevancy:
• Application's name (does it include the keyword)
• Density of the keyword in the description of the application
• Presence of the keyword in the list.

App Annie has created "cheat sheets" to focus on the topmost ASO factors to get discovered and chosen:

Source: App Annie

Figure 6.13 - ASO Essentials

Let us now see in what ways a marketer can influence the main factors:

The average number of stars is a great trust gauge and strongly influences the decision of a user to download an application:

Source: Apptentive

Figure 6.14 – Influence of ratings over download intent

It is, therefore, no surprise that star ratings are a key factor in ranking algorithms. In March 2015, Apptentive found that 98% of free apps in the Google Play top 100 had an average rating of 4 stars or more. Each top-selling app on the App Store has an average of almost 200,000 reviews, and, on Google Play, over 3 million on average.

Unfortunately, only 0.05% of users take the time to write a review for an application. And nearly two-thirds of applications received no stars[40]. The marketer must therefore create a strategy to collect reviews. To make a comment on the Apple App Store, the user must be logged into his iTunes account; on Google Play, comments are all integrated with Google+ to avoid cheating. The algorithm will promote real and active profiles, much like Google's PageRank algorithm gives more weight to links that originate from trusted sites than those from untrusted ones.

However, there are services that you can use at your own risk that provide fake reviews at scale. One can, for example, buy 1,000 positive reviews for a few dollars, or, in a more vicious way, buy 1,000 negative reviews for a competing application. These practices are monitored and not appreciated by App Stores, which can ban guilty applications. The ethical way to accumulate reviews is to create an application that users like, and improve it according to their feedback.

The marketer must carefully choose the right time and the right way to ask a user to write a review. It is recommended to limit request frequency to avoid harassing the user and to ensure that the ask coincides with a positive moment in user experience. For example, a user who has completed their third jogging session may be asked to provide a review for the fitness tracking application they just used. Always respond quickly to user feedback, especially when it's about the application's functionality, bug reporting, or a need for clarification. This demonstrates your responsiveness and your commitment to continue improving the application. Also, do not engage in arguments via commentaries to extoll the pros of your application, and remember that the consumer is always right (it is better to remain silent than to write something derogatory).

One difference between the Apple App Store and the Google Play Store is the possibility for users to vote for an app with a "+1" on Google Play, from its page on Google Play, or from the app itself. This is similar to Facebook's "Like" because it allows users to give a positive review with just one click. These "+1" have an enormous influence on Google Play's algorithm, and, most importantly, they emphasize the fact users think that the app is worth downloading.

VOLUME, RECENCY AND VELOCITY

Even if the actual volume of downloads remains hidden by each platform, it is obvious that it has a major influence on an application's ranking. After all, being in the top 100 chart is equal to having top 100 sales.

---

40 Moz

Without the recency factor, an application that is very well-placed in the rankings would be almost impossible to dethrone (a well ranked application attracts downloads by its visibility, and continues to be ranked thanks to its volume of downloads, forming a virtuous cycle). An application that has accumulated a lot of downloads and positive reviews during its heyday wouldn't then be sensitive to marginal, but significant changes (a lot of negative reviews after an update for example). To prevent this, the algorithms give a disproportionate weight to the most recent information and reviews.

Also, know that the algorithms are programmed to identify trends. For example, an application that is spreading around a very popular event (like applications imitating the Vuvuzela at the 2010 World Cup) will see its ranking improve very quickly. That being said, the denominator remains very large for top ranked apps, which will be less sensitive to volatility.

THE CHOICE OF KEYWORDS

Despite recent changes made to Apple's algorithm, there remains a difference between the two App Stores in terms of keywords and application description.

For iOS applications, developers can provide a list of keywords they would like to be listed for in the keyword field (up to 100 characters). Apple will augment this list with similar words, competitors' names, and app category.

However, this field is not present in the Google Play Store. There, the algorithm analyzes the application's description to identify the keywords that will be used for search results. It is therefore extremely important to include relevant and competitive keywords in the description on Google Play. Note that keyword "stuffing" is strongly sanctioned - it is recommended to repeat target keywords no more than 5 times in the description.

In the App Store, the description of the application has little effect on ranking. But remember that Google's web search engines index iTunes pages. It is therefore important to optimize the description on the App Store with the keywords desired for referencing by Google.

THE FUTURE

One of the major arcs of improvement for App Stores' search algorithms will be to display applications' internal content directly on a search page, thanks to *deep-linking*, or to leverage voice for search and in-app actions (for example, order an Uber from Siri).

STRATEGIC DECISIONS

So, what are the differences between the App Store and Google Play? Although the two competing platforms approach ranking in a similar way, the results differ significantly. The same app can be ranked completely differently in each of the platforms, whether it is a categorization difference and/or a placement difference. Of course, this may be related to the fact that publishers rarely develop parity between the two platforms, preferring to leverage the idiosyncrasies of each one. However, this is also largely influenced by a different list of categories, and a different weight attributed by the algorithm to each of the above factors.

For example, Google Play does not separate reviews by app version, while the App Store does. This factor contributes to creating a much greater volatility of the rankings on the App Store than on Google Play, because it takes a lot of new reviews to change the latter's ranking.

A very important aspect to understand is that ASO is not static but rather a continuous process requiring a lot of time and effort. This is reflected in the need for regular updates and iterations to achieve the best results. Updates can help improve rankings, conversions, downloads, and retention.

Depending on the type of application, competitor strategies and trends, it is recommended to update the ASO every two months. Too frequent updates could potentially handicap the algorithm (keyword indexing usually takes six weeks), affect the ranking and give users a bad impression (for example: changing the name of the application too often could create confusion). However, updating the application every six to eight weeks gives proof to the algorithm that the application is updated and alive. In addition, this will help you test keywords and visuals (closely monitor the impact of the changes). Another benefit of regular updates is that negative reviews from previous versions will be "hidden" on iOS and less accessible, so the average rating will increase if the application has improved.

Of course, don't just update for ASO only. Instead, use the update as an opportunity to renew the application, fix bugs, refresh visuals or implement new features.

The Holy Grail: a feature

Each week, App Stores feature certain applications. In addition to top ranking lists (Top paid apps, Top free apps), App Store editorial teams manually select applications to be featured. Each category, as well as the homepage, has its own featuring opportunities (Top News, Top Trends), and there are also temporary or specific categories for an App Store version. For example, the Hong Kong App Store has a category for local developers. Or, during Valentine's Day, a Romance category will be created. Each of these lists represents an opportunity to be featured. Selected applications will vary from country to country. It is possible to be featured on several categories and/or several countries at once, and the effects compound.

Even though search algorithms' sophistication helps distributing downloads more fairly, getting featured is always the best way to boost downloads. App Annie demonstrates that being featured on the App Store can increase downloads by 25% for non-gaming apps, and 140% for gaming apps![41] This temporary mass influx also contributes to influencing the ranking algorithm, and the benefits of being featured will be felt over the following days, weeks and sometimes months, creating a virtuous circle of improved ranking.

The App Store updates featured applications on Thursdays at noon PST. On Mondays, Apple's editorial team contacts the selected developers to ask them to provide the marketing elements necessary for the promotion. The happy developers can therefore prepare for a massive influx of consumers, with a peak of downloads around Day 3 (during the weekend, typically a period of high demand)[42].

What are the strategies for getting featured? Well, it's impossible to buy one's way in, so one must convince the editorial team. Besides creating a unique and appealing application, it is essential to respect the best practices provided by each App Store. Use the latest App Store features and App Store tools (for example, Game Center for Apple and Google+ for Play Store). Demonstrate respect for the Apple and Google brands (follow the same aesthetic spirit). Localize your application, update it frequently (publish special versions for holidays, for example), and create specific versions for phone, tablet and connected objects, to demonstrate a deep commitment. Any mention in trade press (TechCrunch, Mashable, etc.) improves your chances of being noticed.

---

41 App Annie, *App Store Feature Report*
42 App Annie, *App Store Feature Report*

But often this is not enough to stand out. Being well connected, and building a relationship with the editorial team can have a big impact. It is possible to work with the editorial team to make the changes that it wants before featuring your application. There is a plethora of consultants who promise to get your app featured. The best are those who previously worked in the editorial team of one of the App Stores because they often keep good relationships with them.

Finally, in addition to the downloads provided by being featured, and the resultant improvement in ranking, the developer can hope for more media coverage as bloggers and journalists closely follow the special features of App Stores, which, again, contributes to an increase in volumes.

The right proportions

According to MobyAffiliates, Warc predicts that in 2017, $90 billion dollars will be spent worldwide in mobile advertising. Almost half will go to search engines, and over a third to social media:

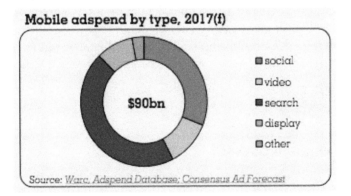

Figure 6.15 - Advertising Expenditure by Type, 2017

This diagram illustrates the overall average, but the share of each distribution channel can vary drastically from one campaign to another. The marketer must evaluate each type of media for its ability to deliver against the objectives of each campaign and decide the budget allocation based on expected results.

In addition, if the publisher is in the launch phase, it will be important to plan a change in volumes and distribution patterns as the campaign progresses. Indeed, at the very beginning, the marketer will cap the budget, and channels, to collect as much performance data as possible before making big decisions. At this stage, the aim is to establish an average CPI, and to validate the KPIs used to calculate the LTV. Then, the marketer will increase the budget on social networks to encourage word-of-mouth. Some may decide to spend a substantial part of the budget in a limited time (a push campaign) in order to boost the ranking algorithm and initiate a virtuous circle. To do this, we've seen earlier in this chapter that incentivized traffic can drive large volumes at a reasonable cost (whatever the user's engagement).

Based on our experience, the campaign budget for a mobile game will be disproportionately allocated to social networks, especially Facebook. Next comes display and video, with a large portion of this expenditure going to Google. The remainder is shared between DSPs and ad networks. Search engines will typically be less important, largely because it's difficult to imagine a typical user scenario: few players will type "find a cool game" in their Google search engine, and even then, good luck to the marketer that tries to be visible on these keywords!

Conversely, a travel app will spend a larger budget on these search engines, and buy all keywords related to destinations, flights, or hotels. On the other hand, their display budget may be proportionally less, as it will be more difficult to build attractive ads for travel destinations on a small mobile banner format.

FACTSHEET

THE PLANNING PROCESS

In practice, it is recommended to prepare a media plan on a quarterly basis and review it monthly. At least every week, the marketer needs to calculate the performance of each distribution channel, in terms of volume, other KPIs and ROI. And then use this information to immediately reallocate budget to the most powerful sources, and optimize, or eliminate, the losers. Often a partner will be unable to deliver the promised volume – be contractually and philosophically prepared to dump them and increase budget elsewhere.

Manage Complexity

"It's incredibly complex in every way. If you want to market at the level we market at, you need well over 100 people just to manage the 300 or 400 ad networks out there in the world. If you want to run television globally it's a gigantic effort."

Gabe Leydon, CEO of MachineZone[43]

The marketer who wants to venture farther than a superficial spend will quickly find himself faced with an unmanageable complexity. Indeed, each media channel has its own advertising formats, its own technologies, and its own needs for optimization and monitoring. The more channels marketers want to test, the more scenarios they will have to manage, with no economies of scale. Most marketers will therefore decide to use agencies or affiliate networks to get the job done. A hybrid approach is recommended:

- It is recommended to keep the most strategic channels (ASO, A/B tests, SEO) under direct control as much as possible;

- Under close supervision, agencies can be used for large and complex channels, such as Facebook and SEM, that require large-scale optimization technologies; but also for newer channels where in-house expertise is lacking (for example a Snapchat channel used for brand exposure);

- Affiliate networks and DSPs provide maximum leverage to discover, manage and optimize small and medium-sized applications, which are hardly worth the effort to approach directly;

The greater the spending in a given channel, the more crucial it is to optimize in real time. For example, a small campaign of a few thousand dollars per month on Facebook can be monitored with little effort. As long as the campaign generates a positive ROI, it is justifiable to spend more money on the channel. Thousands or even tens of thousands of dollars per day are entirely possible on Facebook because the network reaches a huge number of users. At this level, though, the slightest error in the campaign, even the slightest variation in performance, can become very expensive. The marketer will then have to resort to automated technologies and specialized agencies, for example, Nanigans, Kenshoo, KRDS or Ampush, and many others, who are all listed as official partners ("PMD") on Facebook's website.

43 Venture Beat, 2015

FACTSHEET

CHOOSING A PARTNER

Here is some information that will help you in your decisions:

Advertising Agencies
· Advantages: the agency takes care of your campaign from A to Z
· Risks: the agency is paid in proportion to the media budget, so there is an incentive to increase spend with little interest in optimizing performance.

How to choose?
· Only deal with agencies specialized in mobile.
· Weigh the pros and cons of benefiting from special access of large agencies and having to share the spotlight with many other clients (who may have a higher budget), and being the focal point of a small agency, which may be limited in its approach.

Affiliate Networks
· Advantages: Very good knowledge of the market and ability to identify sources of traffic that are inaccessible to most agencies (such as small intermediaries).
· Risks: Paid for installs, these networks may be inclined to obtain installs by any means, for example the use of rewards ("incentives"), or contextual placements on controversial content, with little regard for branding.

How to choose?
· Give preference to networks with a good reputation. Ask for advice! The poor performers are well known.
· Agree on specific criteria for promotion and payment of installations. Take advantage of this conversation to judge the network's transparency.

Technology and Services
· Advantages: Advanced and up-to-date knowledge of major distribution channels. Optimization algorithms and automated campaign creation and management are must-haves for spending large budgets with Google or Facebook.
· Risks: Integration difficulties with existing technologies and risk of not choosing the right tool for the size and type of budget; cost is proportional to the media spend and the number of transactions.

How to choose?
· Define precise specifications and obtain proposals from several suppliers.
· Understand the perimeter of the services included in addition to the technology.
· Organize a test whenever possible.

PARTNERING TIPS AND TRICKS

· Never lose sight of your strategic channels. You must know them by heart. This sometimes means running a few campaigns directly, in parallel to using a partner, to have a basic presence on that channel.
· Demand transparency. Agencies (often due to lack of motivation) and networks (often due to lack of incentive) will offer partial transparency. The larger the budget, the more leverage the marketer has. Stay alert.
· Start networks on a small budget. Measure ROI and all performance indicators before increasing spend.
· Monitor, monitor, monitor:
    - Work with your attribution solution to trace the user journey before download. Verify that visited applications are part of the media plan;
    - Frequently check popular mobile apps and look for advertisements for your app;
    - Check the validity of each download by observing the user's behavior after the installation. Also verify the validity of purchases in your application, as well as the receipt of the amount due.
    - Forewarned is forearmed!

The essentials

- **Google's and Apple's App Stores** are saturated with more than 2 million applications but are both indispensable.

- **ASO, Appstore Search Optimization**, is essential to solving the critical problem of discovery.

- **Multiple App Stores** offer alternate distribution paths, either in an eco-systemic framework (such as Amazon), or independent one (such as Nexway or Yandex).

- **Facebook** is the other major giant of mobile traffic. 20% of the time spent on mobile worldwide is spent on Facebook.

- **Twitter, Snapchat or WeChat** have become central platforms for reaching specific market segments.

- **A very broad range of platforms** is now available to market applications. Their diversity and technical complexity require special marketing skills.

CHAPTER 7

FROM THE CREATIVE TO THE TECHNICAL SIDE

Executive summary

- Mobile marketing has a **deeply creative side** because the marketer can give free rein to their imagination, especially through native formats. Personalization and interactivity reign on this format.

- But it also has a **deeply technical side**, so the marketer must develop the requisite technical skills.

- The marketer who can play on the right and left hemispheres of the mobile user's brain holds all the cards for success.

Mobile, a land of constant innovation, is also a precursor in terms of types and number of advertising formats available. This creates difficulties for marketers, who find themselves having to develop many versions of the same advertisement, each with different sizes and specifications. Two major forces push towards standardization.

On one hand, the cost and time required to create multiple formats forces marketers to choose and focus their efforts on 3 to 5 winning platforms: those that offer not only a fairly large audience, but also high performance formats. We think of Facebook, which, thanks to its dominant size in the mobile advertising market, has managed to impose its formats on the industry. For example, the native format of the Facebook news feed quickly became the most popular native mobile format and was adopted by other major mobile advertising platforms, including Twitter and Cheetah Mobile.

On the other hand, there are two associations of industry professionals working to define standards and best practices. These associations are international, as are their standards. One is the Internet Advertising Bureau (IAB), originally created to set advertising standards for traditional web marketing (versus mobile marketing). The digital boundary between a view from a computer, or a view from a smartphone or tablet, becoming more and more blurred, the IAB has had to "legislate" on mobile display advertising formats. The reference association, however, remains the Mobile Marketing Association (MMA), which was created specifically for mobile media, and explores more than just display, extending to text-based advertising or push notifications.

Display

These associations have published a format recommendation charter for mobile display that has been adopted by the industry, giving the marketer access to a significant inventory (directly from publishers, or through a DSP) using these formats:

FORMAT	SUPPORT	TECHNICAL SPECIFICATIONS
Banner	Smartphone	• 320 x 50 pixels • < 30 kb
	Tablet	• 768 x 90 pixels (Landscape: 1024 x 90 pixels) • < 50 kb
Interstitial	Smartphone	• Portrait: 320 x 480 pixels (Landscape: 480 x 3208 pixels) • < 35 kb
	Tablet	• Portrait: 768 x 1024 pixels (Landscape: 1024 x 768 pixels) • < 100 kb
Recommendations	Smartphone or Tablet	• Image format: .gif, .png, .jpg • Clickable: yes • High resolution: yes (in standard format; ex: Retina, 640x100 banner) • Rich Media/HTML5: yes (ex: MRAID 2.0) • Distinction of advertising character of contents: yes (ex: Tag "AD" to be added if needed) • Interstitial display time: 3 to 5 seconds max and/or close to exit the ad (ex: explicit "press X to close", to be added to the interstitial) • Sound: off at launch

Source: MMA

Figure 7.1 – Main display formats

The most popular display formats are the interstitial (maximum impact but also maximum intrusion, as it is impossible to ignore), and the top (or 320 × 50) horizontal banner format. Dynamic or animated formats must comply with the IAB broadcast standards. The current standard is MRAID 2.0.

The size and placement constraints of display do not make it a very effective format for performance marketing, which aims for a click from the user. It is difficult to cut through banner blindness and engage the consumer to act! Yet, interstitials are still favored by brands because of the belief that repeated exposure may provide an increase in brand awareness, and because this format is the most familiar to agencies.

FACTSHEET

BEST PRACTICES

· Efficiency:
  - To attract the attention of the mobile user, it is better to stand out from the look and feel of the publisher;
  - Use a message that prompts someone to click. For example: "Click to win ...", "Discover the new ... here."; and
  - Think of special and exclusive offers to promote immediate action.

· Clarity:
  - Text: no more than a few words, no complete sentences;
  - Animation: no more than 3 screens; and
  - "Roadblock": The act of buying two or more banners on the same screen. Not recommended on smartphone because it's difficult to execute on a small screen, but possible on tablet. Think about coordinating banners and messages.

Native formats

The limitations of display formats, and the specific possibilities provided by mobile, have rapidly led to the development of native formats specific to mobile.

DEFINITION

The native mobile format, not to be confused with contextual marketing (which targets advertising based on an understanding of adjacent text), is an advertising format that fits perfectly with the application, or mobile site, visited by the user. This can take very different shapes.

As we saw earlier, one of the most popular formats is the "in-stream" or "in-feed" format, which integrates an advertisement in the middle of a news feed, and presents it in the same way as the related news.

DECONSTRUCTION OF A NATIVE FORMAT

Native advertising is typically comprised of several interchangeable elements furnished by the advertiser to the publisher, and automatically placed by the ad service technology used.

Source: MMA

Figure 7.2 – Native format elements

INFINITE POSSIBILITIES

The mobile support allows both publishers and marketers to unleash their creativity and new formats are constantly created. Let's look at these examples:

- "In-stream" (in the news feed): launched by social networks, emulated by news publishers:

Source: MMA

Figure 7.3 – Various in-stream native advertising implementations – news apps

• As well as by m-commerce brands:

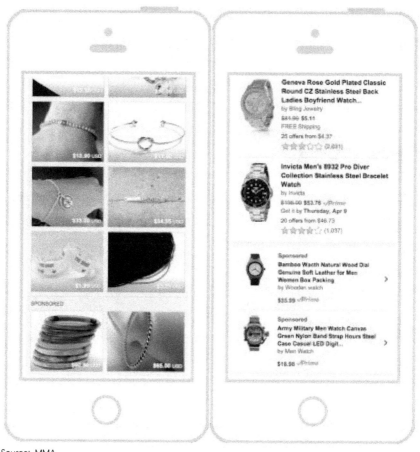

Source: MMA

Figure 7.4 – Various in-stream native advertising implementations – m-commerce apps

• But it is also possible to use mobile-specific functions, such as geolocation, to develop efficient formats centered around geographic search:

Source: MMA

Figure 7.5 – Geo-localized native ads

- Or, to use limited mobile space creatively by rotating several images inside a single advertisement – the "carousel" format. It will be very useful for retailers who want to highlight a selection of their products, brands that want a wider canvas, or those who want to explain a step by step process:

Source: Facebook

Figure 7.6 – Carousel format

- Creativity is unlimited here. Publishers can incorporate immersive advertising into their content. For example, the following game lets American football fans click on the mobile phone that is in the hand of their favorite player to watch a video ad and earn a reward:

Source: MMA

Figure 7.7 – Immersive native format

Or this news publisher which inserts advertising for applications in a section devoted to article recommendations.

Source: MMA

Figure 7.8–Native recommendation format

THE MOBILE NATIVE'S GUIDE TO MARKETING

- Or, finally, the publisher that creates a feature that is an ad, or an ad that is also useful, depending upon your point of view: Cheetah Mobile offers a lock screen that can be completely transformed into advertising:

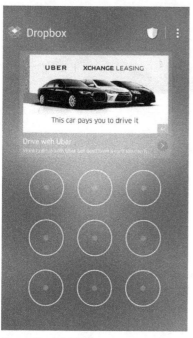 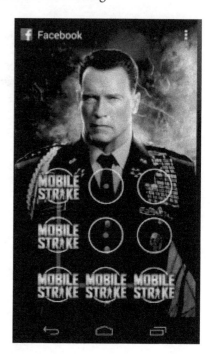

Source: Cheetah Mobile

Figure 7.9 – Lock screen ad

Because native formats provide an infinite substrate for the creativity of marketers and publishers, they are hard to scale. Indeed, the lack of standards and almost infinite possibilities amount to creating advertisements for single use: one visual per publisher. For the advertiser with an appetite for growth, this generates a dramatic cost of creation and a significant management complexity. This explains why, despite their superior performance in terms of KPIs and consumer satisfaction, native formats remain infrequent in mobile. This rarity is reinforced by the fact that few mobile DSPs offer access to native formats (again, due to the lack of standardization). My prediction is that the industry will hone in on a few winning formats (e.g. the Facebook in-stream format), and technologies will emerge to dynamically create native ads from modular standard elements. In the meantime, marketers should focus on market leaders with significant inventory to ensure any creative investment is worthwhile.

BEYOND THE FORMAT

Native advertising strategy should not be restricted to format alone. Fundamentally, the goal of native advertising is to perfectly integrate in the user experience, and to elicit an engagement superior to a traditional banner. This is only possible by mastering two other factors: relevance and timing. Indeed, even advertising that is both appealing and well integrated in an app will be perceived as intrusive if it is poorly targeted.

A mobile native marketing campaign should thus respect the following three components:

- Creative and mobile-optimized **format**;
- Perfect **timing**; and
- Successful **targeting**.

We've already established that, creatively, everything is possible with native formats. Now, let's explore now how to achieve perfect timing, starting with a counter-example. Think of a user who wants to start her day by meditating. She downloads a meditation app, opens it to select the duration of her meditation, and there appears an ill-timed advertisement for an energy drink. It is not the right moment for this ad! This is annoying to the user, a disastrous experience for the publisher (who will be lucky if the user does not immediately decide to uninstall its app), and leaves a bad impression of the brand -- the opposite of the desired effect.

The better approach would be for the publisher to judiciously identify moments of natural breaks in the user experience, during which the user is mentally available and receptive. For example, at the end of the meditation, it would be savvy to advertise that drink and help the user tackle the day ahead. The brand would then be associated with the positive feeling of having completed a meditation session and starting the day fresh and energized.

The concept of optimal timing is also linked to the recent experience of the user. Mobile collects much more contextual information about a user than any other medium. Take, for example, a business woman who travels. Classical DMPs would put her in this targeting category all the time. But she is not traveling all the time. So, if HotelTonight, a brand offering discounts on same-day hotel reservations, wanted to recruit this user, would it not be much more effective to target her when her mobile phone detects that she is on the move, or at an airport? This kind of data, dynamic and in near real time, is available on the main mobile platforms.

By following these three principles, native advertising not only attracts the attention of the user, but also develops a favorable brand opinion, and begins to engage the user at first sight. A well-executed native format can deliver an engagement rate 20-60% higher than traditional banners, and a retention rate 3x greater. Due to its effectiveness, this format is one of the most popular today, and IHS.Inc predicts that it will account for more than 60% of global mobile marketing investments in 2020[1].

Video

Mobile video views are booming. It goes without saying that video is also a very effective advertising medium on mobile. Whether played in a news stream (an "*in-stream*" native format), or "*out-stream*", that is to say inside a banner (often through a DSP that specializes in video, such as SpotX), or as a "*pre-roll*" video trailer, mobile video is attractive to marketers, who want a format that is familiar (after all, many marketers have been trained at the school of television advertising), and allows for rich storytelling. Successful mobile video advertising follows these best practices:

- **Get attention quickly.** Stimulating people's interest quickly has become a necessity for video content, especially on mobile devices. Create short stories that captivate your audience. Design content for mobile, do not use a TV ad straight up!
- **Start your video** with captivating images of your products, action items, and a striking background. Use colors, themes and images that evoke your brand from the start, so that people quickly associate the ad with your brand.
- **Create a soundless video.** Since most mobile video ads will run in-stream and will start without sound, it is essential to express your message visually. The integration of subtitles, your logo, and products, help to convey your message even when sound is off.
- **Frame your story.** Think of how to of adapt the dimensions of your video for smartphones, taking into account both the reduced size and verticality of the screen. Play with the zoom, the frame and the overall visual composition to guarantee a quality story on this medium. In particular, plan close-ups and a large font size for any writing.

---

1 Marketing Land

It is strongly recommended to adhere to IAB standards for video: VAST (modalities of interaction between the ad server and the video player), and VPAID (modalities of interaction between the video player and the content of the news feed). These standards allow the marketer to keep control over visuals and interchange, or rotate, them automatically.

FACTSHEET

VIDEO FORMAT

The video format is by far one of the most expensive to create. The savvy marketer will therefore take care to create modular videos that can be used on different media, and for different occasions, with only re-cutting work, and without having to re-film. For example, it is possible to create a video ad for television, and plan from the beginning how it will be re-cut for mobile, and subtitles added. Vertical video formats are essential on mobile, especially on Snapchat. If you want to use this network, it is imperative to create a vertical video first, rather than trying to force the consumer to turn their screen.

What about tablets?

The smartphone is everywhere, while tablets remains limited to specific categories and demographic groups. While the use of tablets increases with the age of consumers, it remains less than the time spent on smartphones. Many advertisers do not develop a tablet-specific application: either users zoom in on the smartphone app, or they use a "responsive" version of the mobile website. However, it is not the same for advertising formats. Remember to check the rendering of your images on a larger screen. And remember that tablets are less easy to reorient than smartphones: a vertical video, perfect for a smartphone, will not be appreciated by tablet users.

Best practices

PACKING IMPACT IN A SMALL FORMAT

To attract the attention of a busy, multitasking consumer on the move, it is necessary to be eye catching. On a mobile screen, formats are small. Simple, colorful, immediately identifiable images attract the eye. Those that intrigue the consumer can make him click – though it is important not to frustrate the user by being too mysterious: patience is very limited on mobile.

To this point, choose very explicit and descriptive images. Consider, for example, how the developer of the game *Fantasy Chronicles* provides a gameplay scene in an advertisement on Facebook, making us want to discover more:

Source: Nanigans, The Performance Marketer's Guide to Scaling Growth

Figure 7.10 – *Fantasy Chronicles* advertising on Facebook

Games lend themselves perfectly to the video format, simulating the game play, and making the consumer want to try it. By animating game sequences, the developer illustrates their product effectively, and produces video at a lower cost (far cheaper than producing a television spot). This allows for many variations (localization of language by country, tests of various creative concepts, etc.), and the ability to frequently refresh ads with new content.

The carousel format is perfect for m-commerce pros, who can use it to entice users with the richness of their catalog. In more advanced cases, this format can be used to dynamically present products of specific interest to the user during a retargeting campaign. Facebook measured a cost reduction of up to 50% using this format.

Source: Facebook

Figure 7.11 – Carousel format on Facebook

RAPIDLY ADOPTING NEW FORMATS

Mobile game developers tend to be pioneers in terms of adopting new ad formats. Recently Nanigans found that its customers in this category had adopted the video and carousel formats launched by Facebook, Instagram and Twitter in less than six months:

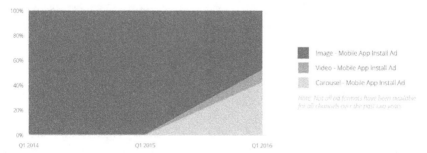

Source: Nanigans, *The Performance Marketer's Guide to Scaling Growth with Mobile App Installs Ads*, 2016.

Figure 7.12 – Mobile app install spend by format (among Nanigans clients on Facebook, Instagram and Twitter)

"Ad-blockalypse"?

The very rapid rise of ad blockers has been debated in specialized press and at conferences. While ad blockers are far from being as popular on mobile as on desktop, their large adoption and impact on the latter warrants close examination of any uptick in the former. Recently, Apple has allowed ad blockers to run on their mobile browser, Safari, causing the launch of many ad blocking applications, and a fast growth of projections of ad block rates on mobile. Currently low in Western countries (despite a high sensitivity to privacy in European countries like France or Germany), this rate is already high in India and China (9% and 8% respectively). UC Browser and Maxathon, which offer an ad blocker on Android, are very popular browser options internationally.

The consumer who blocks ads is actually the ideal consumer for many brands and publishers - a technophile, a consumer of mobile content, young and male – a typically elusive target that just became harder to reach.

Apart from the risk for publishers, whose advertising revenue is a main source of income, ad blockers send a very strong signal for marketers: the public is tired of intrusive ads! For the moment, ad blockers only work on mobile sites, and not on apps. However, this is bound to change. Marketers would do well to evolve voluntarily before technology forces them to.

This technology was precisely created as a reaction to troubles emanating from digital advertising abuses – intrusive, inopportune and irrelevant ads. The fact is, ad blocking is an obstacle resulting from the lack of creativity of marketers. For a long time, we failed to find the most effective tools to interact with users, who then got impatient and found a way to block us. My position is that marketers should not be wary of ad-blockers, they should embrace them, as a forcing factor to improve. It's good when users communicate what they like and do not like. This enables the advertising industry to evolve. Creativity improves, and our ability to deliver targeted messages at the right time is perfected. Of course, this does not mean that the road ahead will be easy.

Seen from a positive angle, the blocking of advertisements is a sign that mobile marketing is reaching maturity. There is a huge audience of mobile users who are becoming more sophisticated, and are willing to be engaged and satisfied. All marketers and advertisers need to do is to offer a real benefit to the consumer, at the right time.

Test, test, test and localize

While testing different versions of an application requires specialized software (as we will see later), creative and campaign testing is embedded in most tools already used for marketing campaigns. This must be leveraged!

Ad servers, partners and publishers must be able to rotate different versions of their visuals, whatever they are. Marketers should demand performance reports that compare click-through rates, conversion rates and ultimately, ROI, by creative and campaign types.

More complex tests that allow for variations of multiple elements at the same time (e.g. finding the winning combination of 3 image versions, 5 call-to-action verbs, and 4 text versions) require specialized tools, such as AdBasis, that use statistical methods to save test cycles, and help marketers get to optimal versions more quickly.

It is important to consider the volume of distribution of your visuals (the media buy size) before undertaking any test. Assume it will require a certain number of interactions to obtain statistical validity. If you want to optimize for the best ROI, this volume of interaction can be important: for example, with a 1% CTR, a 10% CVR (installation rate), and an action rate (say, a sale) of 20% the first week, you will have to reach 500,000 impressions per visual version to collect 100 sales per visual (500,000 × 1% × 10% × 20%). If you test 4 versions at the same time, you will need to buy 2 million impressions. At $10 CPM, you will have spent a budget of $20,000 for this test.

To optimize your budget, program your tests by phase. First find the best CTR – which you can obtain in about 200-300,000 impressions, then create new variations of these visuals to optimize CVR and ROI. It's cheaper to test new concepts on banners first, before implementing them in native and video formats.

As a rule, consider that any marketing budget spent buying media should have a certain percentage dedicated to testing. This way, you can continuously improve and refresh visuals, and achieve performance improvements immediately.

Finally, if you want to distribute your application abroad, even if you do not localize the application (e.g. a simple game can remain in English at the beginning), it is still important to localize advertising! To control costs, concentrate your efforts on the banners at first.

Deep-linking

DEFINITION

A deep link is a link that takes you straight to the target content. Most web links are deep links. For example, *https://www.appannie.com/en/apps/ios/top/* is a deep link. On the other hand, *http://www.appannie.com* is not a deep link, as it simply takes you to the App Annie home page.

In its simplest form, deep linking allows users to share content that is in an application.

If you want to send your friend the link to App Annie's top iOS apps report, you can do it using a deep link to the App Annie application. Without this, your friend will have to open the App Annie application, and search for it.

HOW DOES IT WORK?

There is no standard for *deep linking*, but generally a good system contains the following:

- A URL scheme for each application (so that each page has a unique address);
- A smart redirect to the App Store if the user has not already installed the application; and
- The ability to pass and save user-specific settings, such as an individual promotion code, or the user's date and time of arrival.

Several companies, such as Branch.io, are pushing to establish standards on the marketplace and allow a greater fluidity between applications.

HOW TO USE IT?

Deep linking is an essential part of any mobile marketing campaign. It is particularly important in the following cases:

- Promotion of a product or type of product (m-commerce, travel, home delivery, etc.): conversion rate is multiplied and user experience greatly improved by the use of deep linking (see HotelTonight case study);

M-COMMERCE

Without deep linking:

The flower shop Interflora launches a mobile marketing campaign for Mother's Day. The ads promote an assortment of bouquets for moms. The user searches on Google "Flowers for Mom." He clicks on an advertisement from Interflora, and is directed to the App Store. But he already has the app installed, so the user clicks to open it, then is taken to the home screen of the application, where he must resume the search for bouquets for Mother's Day.

With deep linking:

The user clicks from the Google search results page and is transported directly to the Mother's Day bouquet page on the Interflora application. This saves two steps, and avoids losing and frustrating many users.

- Re-targeting: when targeting a user who has abandoned a shopping cart, it is imperative to send the user directly to the product they were interested in, rather than to a generic home page or back to the App Store;

- Transitioning mobile internet users to the application: when you encourage users of your mobile internet sites to download your application, let them continue their navigation exactly where they left off.

HOTEL TONIGHT

Hotel Tonight is a booking application for last-minute hotel rooms. This company has commissioned Branch.io to improve the ROI of their marketing campaigns. Indeed, the performance of their SEM campaigns did not enable them to pay competitive prices in this highly competitive category. The loss of users between clicking (paying) on advertising and booking a room was too great. By implementing deep linking through Branch.io, Hotel Tonight ensured that its users reached the content they requested, by the shortest path possible. The result was a 16% reduction in the CPI, and an 18% increase in reservation rate, allowing Hotel Tonight to increase their mobile SEM budget with confidence.

On the wise use of targeting data

A NEEDLE IN A HAYSTACK

Too much data kills information: to date, there are about 2 billion mobile internet users on the planet. As you can imagine, all this activity produces an enormous amount of data, each application potentially containing behavioral information of inestimable value to advertisers. The problem is that mobile users are generating so much data that it is extraordinarily difficult for anyone to make sense of it all.

For example, one day, an exasperated mom downloads Candy Crush to keep her children busy at the supermarket checkout line. This information is stored in DMPs. Unfortunately, mom isn't the player, so any marketer trying to promote a competing game to her will be wasting their time.

It is therefore necessary to focus on the signals that indicate the user's intention. But how does one identify them in this gigantic haystack?

First, primary data should be favored. This is a reliable data set, either because it is the data in your proprietary database (i.e. Uber can identify most popular zip codes for route requests and target those for new customer acquisition), or because the user herself is the editor of the data (e.g. Facebook profiles). Source data quality has an enormous impact on targeting quality. Much data purchased from a third party is completely outdated. For example, a user could at one time sign up on a dating application. This information was saved in a DMP, and he is categorized as single. He has since met the love of his life, who probably will not be very happy to see dating ads on his phone! Updating data is therefore paramount.

Behavioral data should be preferred over demographic profiles. Most consumers share their demographic information with very few applications or mobile sites, yet all advertising platforms seem to provide this targeting option. In reality, many marketing platforms base their demographic profiling on assumptions. Take the example of a female user of a poker game. Generally, this is an activity that publishers associate with men. So, if you use third-party data to target ads for your new gambling application, the technology will probably assume that this user is a male and serve her male-targeted creatives, for example one with a buxom girl. This may fail miserably. Since you have no visibility in this black box, or any indication of the origin of the targeting data, you will not know why it did not work.

There are several applications that trace (or *"sniff"*) all applications downloaded and used on your phone. Some do by design, such as battery saving apps, while some do it in an unacknowledged way, for example a VPN app. Confessed or not, the goal is to group users into rich profiles, finding the intersection between the users of Uber, Candy Crush and Expedia. Some platforms may also know the types of ads to which a user is are receptive (which apps were downloaded after seeing an ad?). Others, such as Facebook, have integrated tracking solutions that can even see the LTV a user represents for their advertisers. One can imagine the possible optimization capabilities.

< FOCUS >

DATA VERIFICATION

Nielsen Digital Ad Ratings, ComScore, Mobile Metrix, Integral Ad Science, or Double Click Verification are among the recommended tools for validating demographic and sociological data. Unfortunately, in addition to the added cost, these tools are quite recent on mobile and are not available on all platforms.

Additionally, position data (GPS) is notoriously false and difficult to verify. Location is often comprised of a cocktail of data points. When an app is open and location services are activated the app begins to try to understand where the individual is. The app gives an approximation of the location, which becomes clearer over time (that's why when you open Google Maps, you first see a large blue circle that shows where the individual is located, and it slowly becomes a tighter blue dot when the application has finished triangulating Wi-Fi data, cell phone tower,

GPS, etc.) However, precision does not mean accuracy: indeed, the notion of location is transient. The consumer is always on the move. Location data obtained a few hours ago might be completely useless - but the marketer has no visibility on the freshness of the data they get from a DSP. Moreover, there are myriad ways to lose precision. For example, GPS coordinates can be truncated. The GPS signal can "jump" from a tower to another, making the user appear one second on top of the Empire State Building and the next on Broadway. For fine-toothed targeting, the marketer will therefore be careful to ask specific questions to their data provider. Finally, there will be less error using geolocation data to create user segments (for example, all those who go to the park on Sundays) because the number of data points will drown individual errors.

PREDICTIVE TARGETING - ANTICIPATING NEEDS

A few years ago, an American photographer traveling in Tokyo, saw an electronic billboard with the message "Hello Jim, we have the Nikon lens you're looking for in this store!" The brilliant marketer behind this tactic had combined the recognition of Jim's mobile phone number with a web search that had identified his photography blog, detailing Jim's confessed desire to buy a new Nikon lens.

This is an example of perfect targeting: reaching the right consumer, in the right place, and at the exact moment the consumer's need arises. Technologically, it is now possible to anticipate the needs of consumers based on logic. For example, one can imagine that a user who has just finished recording a jogging session on Runtastic may be thirsty. This would be a perfect time to show her an advertisement for the Gatorade brand. By correlating this information with GPS position, and offering a discount coupon on a drink from the nearest supermarket, you get near perfect targeting.

A scenario that is easy to implement at scale is to use external information to modify marketing campaigns dynamically. For example, a weather application can offer advertisers the ability to update visuals dynamically based on the weather forecast. Is it going to rain in Seattle? Use the visual that shows the umbrellas. It's hot in L.A.? Show a refreshing mist.

In theory, using artificial intelligence to mine billions of signals, some companies promise to be able to anticipate the user's needs based on their recent behavior. Applications that track app usage (for example a battery saving app, but also potentially Facebook or Google), know what applications are used, when and how long. On this basis, the marketer may in theory observe that a user, fond of mobile games, is getting tired of a competing game, and target the user with their own.

Although theoretically possible, these scenarios require access to an astronomical amount of data (i.e. a very large audience), the ability to analyze that data in real time and extract relevant and useful information for the marketer, all while preserving the privacy of users. To this end, the use of "Big Data" in marketing is growing quickly.

WHO, WHAT, WHEN, WHERE, WHY?

Let's not forget targeting specific to mobile. Very often, it is possible to know if an individual is connected through a Wi-Fi network, or a GSM network. This knowledge allows one to postpone an ad until the user has the required bandwidth. It is also possible to know, in a certain number of cases, which telephone network the user is on, sometimes leading to socio-economic assumptions (for example, a user of pre-paid phone cards often has a modest budget). Finally, geolocalization has long been the promised land for mobile marketing. In the five questions of marketing (who, what, when, where, why), mobile was supposed to offer the answer to "where". The vision was: "We will use your GPS, or a beacon, or Wi-Fi and our app will know that you are nearby and send you an advertisement for our shop." The problem with this line of thought is that it interprets location for circumstance. A consumer can walk the same pavement twice a day on their daily commute, but that does not mean they would like to go into the local Starbucks every time. Sometimes he may be late for a business meeting, sometimes he may want to bring coffee for his whole team. The marketer must think beyond the simplistic "We're here, you're near, come and buy from us." It is not enough to find the user; they must be found at the right time, and in the right frame of mind.

EXAMPLE

Let's look at two brands that use geolocation in their marketing plans:

· Walgreens dynamically modifies their application according to where the individual is. For example, if the user walks on the street and opens his app, the first thing it shows him is a store locator. But, if this individual is inside a Walgreens store, he no longer needs to locate one, so the application opens to a different page, such as a reminder to retrieve a prescription. This is interesting because Walgreens not only demonstrates the technical intelligence needed to switch between two types of localization technologies (GPS and beacons), but also because they are able to use this data to dynamically adapt the experience of their application according to the fluctuating circumstances of the user.

· Waze is an application that helps avoid traffic jams, using participatory production (each user shares his position, speed, and indications of problems or slowdowns on the road) to calculate the fastest way to get to from point A to point B. Users appreciate the application for its convenience and the precious minutes saved on their daily commutes. That being the case, what to make of an ad for a $1 coupon to a coffee shop requiring them to take a 15-minute detour? Is a user who just used Waze to shave 5 minutes off of their commute really interested in spending 15 more to save a dollar? Doubtful. Waze has probably come to a similar conclusion because they offer the (weak) option of saving the offer for later. This example demonstrates that the most accurate geographic targeting is useless if user experience is not understood in context.

How could a consumer brand benefit from geolocation? Most American consumers do not download either CPG applications, or retailer applications. So, it's impossible to use push notifications to contact the shopper while in store. The more likely experience is that the consumer is using a messaging application, such as Facebook or iMessage, during their shopping trip: "Honey, do we still have chips at home? Did the children eat?" A brand that wants to attract attention in this context could advertise at that moment in the messaging application, by using precise position as defined by a beacon or the like.

Smartphones accompany users 24 hours a day, 7 days a week. They contain a wealth of behavioral and personal data, so users' expectations about the type of ads and the content they receive are high. The informal contract between publishers, advertisers and users is that they will share their data if they receive equivalent value in return. In my opinion, this applies to advertising as well.

In summary, the marketer's dream of having personal conversations with each individual is within reach, but it requires a lot of sophistication and control over the data sources used.

WHY AUDIENCE EXPANSION MATTERS MORE THAN RE-TARGETING

The scenario is familiar: the consumer goes online and looks at a mixer, camera, or perhaps a new handbag, and for days afterwards, the images of these articles follow her everywhere on the internet, regardless of the website she visits.

This is retargeting in its purest form i.e., the act of identifying lost consumers, anyone who visited your application or website without making a purchase, and trying to convince them to do it a few days or hours later, often by using a special offer. In the physical world, this would mean pursuing a consumer who left your store through the streets, shouting at him to come back.

This idea is not so crazy in the digital world, where transactions are often interrupted by an untimely text message, some distraction, or simply the end of the bus route. In the field of e-commerce, companies like Criteo have built an empire on retargeting, allowing some e-commerce players to increase their revenues by 10%.

The technical impossibility of using cookies on mobile slowed down the arrival of retargeting on this medium, but the purchase of AdX by Criteo and many other similar transactions marked the resolution of the technical difficulties. However, mobile retargeting has not yet delivered results at scale. Why?

The search for these lost users is a Herculean task in the mobile world. Indeed, it is necessary to have a large list of users to target for each type of product. It is recommended to get at least 100,000 users. In addition, it is necessary to have their GAID or IDFA, to find them elsewhere, as well as to integrate this data with information about the product that interested them in the first place. This list must be constantly updated, with the probability of convincing the user decreasing hour by hour. The risk is that, by the time the marketer puts all that together, the consumer has bought their shoes elsewhere. The volume of transactions of many m-commerce companies is simply too small to draw a sufficiently large group. Or they may not have the technical ability to retrieve this information in real time.

After that, there is still the need to create a campaign and advertisements for each product or product type (there's no point offering black city shoes to someone looking at red sports shoes). Each of these campaigns must then be uploaded to a DSP.

Finally, the *coup de grace* will be the ability to find this user in fractions of seconds, on an app or a mobile site that can shows banner ads (retargeting is currently much easier in banners than in native formats), and the ability to win the competition for that impression. Add it all up and, mathematically at least, the probability for success is low.

Conversely, an audience extension campaign uses the same type of data to grow the pie. The principle is to identify the best consumers and to look for consumers with a similar profile. The benefits are many. The identification of the core target can be carried out in delayed time, and the expansion process typically generates a target of significant size.

This work of profile matching makes it possible to increase the size of the audience to the point that it becomes much more frequently found on an application, or a mobile site. This makes it less competitive to acquire a particular user, limiting the cost of auction, and allowing you to grow a core audience from tens of thousands of users, to potentially millions. Clearly, the revenue potential of this type of campaign is likely to exceed that of the retargeting campaigns.

The keystone of this process is the algorithm for identifying similar users. Its quality will determine the quality of your target. A good algorithm will make some assumptions based on the characteristics of the core target (e.g. Do these users tend to have Groupon installed? Does the core target tend to use texting applications every day? What is their demographic composition?). Once these questions are answered, the algorithm can fetch some similar users according to the criteria in its database, and test your ad. If a target cohort responds more favorably than the average, it will be added to the core audience. Otherwise the correlation criteria will be reviewed, and the tests will start again.

This technique is in vogue with the DSPs and with Facebook, who has made it one of its spotlight features.

Mobile ad tech: the tools of the marketer

TRACKING

In a world where cookies are unreliable, the marketer's best friend is a good tool for tracking and attributing downloads. It is important that this tool uses several identification methods that complement each other:

- A unique advertising identifier provided by Apple (IDFA), or Google (GAID);
- A "fingerprint", or proprietary combination of IP address, date and time, origin, etc., making it possible to recognize a user with a certain probability; and/or
- A cookie, in the case of mobile websites.

Technologies are mature, and most tools offer many other services:

- In-app tracking, or monitoring user behavior and path in the application;
- LTV estimation;
- ROI calculation, by media source, campaign, creative, etc.;
- App Store ranking;
- Comparison of ASO with competing applications;
- Etc.

The best-known solutions are Tune, Kochava, Adjust, and Appsflyer. They must be implemented in the application beforehand, via their Software Development Kit (SDK).

Today, the crux of mobile attribution innovation is around the attribution windows, and partial allocations. First, the industry has adopted a 7-day standard to attribute a download to a media source, except Facebook, which claims any download generated for 30 days after a user clicked on an advertisement on the social network – this will prompt experienced marketers to ask if ROI on Facebook is overestimated. Second, it often happens that several media channels contribute to the conversion of a user.

The user may have seen a banner for the Wish application when she was playing Candy Crush. In a rush to continue playing, she closes it. The next day, she wants to shop and opens her Google Search engine, types "Wish shopping app" and clicks on the advertisement for the application. This download must be credited to both Google and Candy Crush in accurate proportions, in order to calculate ROI correctly.

In the future, allocation will include the user's path through various devices: from the physical world (through connected objects, or beacons), to the computer, the smartphone, connected televisions, and the tablet. Solutions must continue to develop their capabilities to integrate new signals, and develop new technologies and partnerships to identify users regardless of their device.

ENGAGEMENT, TESTING AND OPTIMIZATION

The need to retain users, maximize ROI by improving their path through the application, and communicate with them, balanced against the relative difficulty of launching an app update, have created a market for tools to optimize user experience. Two categories of features are covered: analysis of user behaviors and optimization or testing of different versions. To survive in a fast-paced world - and success is linked to responsiveness - it is imperative that these tools be directly accessible to marketers, without resorting to technical resources (e.g. engineering). In a world where retention rate can make or break a campaign's ROI, it makes sense to invest time, money and resources in these tools.

User behavior analysis helps define key moments of the application and the corresponding KPIs to measure. For example, which sections of the application are most successful? More specifically, what product? Where do users come from? On what platform are they? Which features are popular? Let's take the example of a photography application. The marketer will be able to analyze whether the editing feature is used more than the filter feature. They will also be able to see if users acquired through word of mouth are more engaged than those acquired through paid media. And if users on iPad share photos three times more than those on an Android smartphone. Thanks to these tools, powerful insights are at the fingertips of the marketer.

A/B testing tools help create modified versions of an app and make them available only for certain audiences (either a control group and a test group, or a specific category of user: for example, buyers only, or new users only). Once the versions have been used by enough consumers, the marketer will be able to compare KPIs, engagement and monetization.

These tools, although similar to those available for the internet, require different technology; for example, tracking of users differs enormously (no cookies). The user path is also very different from a website: fewer links between pages, shorter pages, critical importance of a "main path" for monetization, etc. Finally, the connectivity of mobile phones is often bad, so it is important to find a tool that is optimized for reduced bandwidth so as not to slow down experience. To satisfy these criteria, I recommend using an A/B testing and optimization software specifically designed for mobile. Apptimize, LeanPlum, Mixpanel, and others are good choices here.

In addition, the logical extension of analyzing user behavior is to modify the application accordingly. For example, the marketer will want to be able to test the best time to present a request for review (on the App Store). Is it after the third screen? The fifth? Does this vary by type of user, or path? In this market, analysis, optimization and engagement software (like push notifications tools) are becoming more and more integrated, either through organic product development or through acquisition. Localytics, Appboy or Urban Airship are notable players in this realm.

For each tool we have reviewed, appropriate parameterization is paramount to deriving the best value.

TIPS TO SAVE TIME

· Always check that the SDK does not crash the application. It happens more often than you would think! Many tools offer free versions, so use them;

· In addition to comparing functionality, it is advisable to compare efficacy of optimization algorithms. For example, will the algorithm be able to distinguish noise from a statistically proven signal? Trying one tool after another is imperfect (any good comparison must be done under similar conditions), and it is expensive to jump from one technology to another. Focus on 2 tools maximum for final tests. If possible, test them on two comparable versions of the application, at the same time;

· Prefer tools that let you select KPIs after implementation. It is virtually impossible to imagine all interesting measurement scenarios in advance;

· It is better to have a tool that offers the fluidity of a single click between concept, test and distribution of the version with the best performance rate;

· Invest in access to specialized knowledge, either in the form of support and advice from the chosen software company, or by hiring a consultant, preferably a statistician. Many A/B tests (regardless of the platform) fail because they have been incorrectly set up; and

· Keep ownership of data, and keep control over the user path. Always have the means to extract data and easily replicate the user path in a future tool. Of course, that's easier said than done.

ANTONY FABY
Senior Producer, Gameloft

Mobile gaming has become the equivalent of a retail store: get people in for free, and try to convert as many visitors as possible. The resulting marketing strategy has two steps: the game must be designed differently to adapt to this constraint, and once it is live, it is necessary to optimize according to the data collected.

HOW DOES MOBILE MARKETING INFLUENCE MOBILE GAMING?

From the development phase of a game, we will ensure that our tracking system is fine enough to be able to analyze and adjust the right parameters. We must however not fall in the trap of tracking too much: collecting too much data would not be useful, because it would become too difficult to separate the noise from the signal.

In the same way, it is during development that we will define the "pointcuts" and "matchers" that will form the basis of our CRM. The goal is to display targeted promotions, based on the activity of the player. For example, if a user loses several times at a given level, we will be able to offer him a promotion to buy a special power that would allow him to finish the level more easily.

The CRM is also useful for dynamically adjusting items displayed in the game shop. This is where the game's internal currency will be sold (for real money). It is therefore crucial that this "shop" is always customized to the needs of the player.

For example, if the player frequently spends more than $50 per purchase, he or she will be offered a promotion on an item at $100 to turn them into bigger spenders.

Finally, the CRM will be used to reward "loyal" players, either because they have reached a particular level of the game or because they have connected frequently during the last few days. They will be offered a small virtual gift to encourage them to continue to be loyal. Another method to reward the loyalty of the players is a VIP system. The idea is very simple: the more a spends in the game, the more his VIP status improves. This will give him access to privileges (for example, an exclusive game character) from which "regular" players are excluded. This system therefore strengthens the loyalty of paying players, and encourages non-paying players to convert.

Other tools are also set up very early to keep the attention of players. This includes the design of push notifications; these are reminder messages that will appear in the main menu of the user's phone, even if the game is closed. For example, if the player has not opened the game for several days, we will invite him to come back and play via a notification, offering him a gift if he does so immediately. It is a critical tool for retention, and unfortunately too often forgotten or misused by developers.

Apart from these elements, the main way to keep players engaged once the game is live, goes through 2 main levers. The first is to continuously offer new content through free upgrades (often, community features). The second is to offer limited time events such as, for example, a 2-day tournament.

However, whatever one does for in-game marketing, the best tool to engage and then monetize the players will be to offer a quality and fun experience.

AD SERVER: BRAND CONTROL

Brands purchasing CPM impressions will want to control the presentation of their identity and the validity of the impressions. Brands and their agencies will work with an independent ad server such as Medialets, Double Click (bought by Google), or Atlas (bought by Facebook) to verify that the impressions have been delivered. Additionally, by using these ad servers, the brand retains control over what visuals are displayed and where they are broadcast, without any risk that the publisher or subcontractors alter the visuals and identity of the mark. These ad servers are integrated into major mobile marketing platforms, which accept their numbers for invoicing.

ALLISON SCHIFF
Senior Editor at AdExchanger

MOBILE VENDORS HAVE AN 'IDENTITY CRISIS' – AND IT'S LEAVING ADVERTISERS A BIT CONFUSED

In today's mobile ad tech landscape, the blind lead the blind.

That's according to Forrester in a report released [in December 2014] that aims to help advertisers get some clarity into what's become an immature and murky market of mobile vendors.

Most mobile tech players aren't clear enough about the services they provide, often using jargon and buzzwords that obfuscate their offerings – but it's not just the vendors who are to blame.

"Marketers aren't exactly sure what to ask for from their partners, which is why vendors are trying to be the answer to any possible question," said Forrester research analyst Jennifer Wise, who penned the report. "If you want cross-channel, the vendor will say, 'We do cross-channel.' If you want online to offline, they'll say they do

that, too. If you need help creating a new mobile format, they're there.

"The bottom line is that everyone will tell you that they can do everything."

And it's holding the market back.

Less than a third of the 35 mobile ad tech vendors surveyed by Forrester are what Wise referred to as "purebreds," meaning that the majority of vendors don't identify with a single core offering. Roughly one-fifth of the vendors claimed that their capabilities span the veritable gamut at equal parts DSP, SSP, ad network, server and exchange.

While some of that can be attributed to consolidation in the market, in-house development or, simply, as the result of opportunistic – or, shall we say, proactive – positioning, the fact remains that many marketers aren't sure how to go about selecting the right mobile ad partner.

"It's true that advertisers are spoiled for choice – they do have a lot of it – but the core problem is not that they have their pick, but that they don't know *how* to choose because they're picking their way through jargon," Wise said. "That's why we're calling on advertisers to optimize for mobile specifically, because mobile is and should be very different than whatever they're doing for display."

In other words, the onus is on marketers to ask the right questions and start educating themselves about the mobile space, rather than just continuing to work with whoever they work with for display because it's convenient or because they assume their vendor knows what it's doing.

Advertisers also need to have a clearer idea of their own goals and KPIs at the outset before grabbing onto a passing mobile vendor and shooting off into an uncertain mobile future like Marty McFly on his skateboard in "Back To The Future."

"It's easy to get lost in the jargon and think, 'This sounds great,' but it's time for advertisers to take charge, understand their own requirements first and even get into the tech a little, too," Wise

said. " How does a particular vendor connect the online digital consumer to the store? Are they using a unique ID like an email address or are they using device location? What kind of inventory do they have access to? Ask."

It's about due diligence, especially in key areas such as creative capabilities, targeting granularity, inventory access and global footprint, as well as a vendor's pricing models and any additional services and add-ons, like measurement, attribution or cross-device.

"A more informed conversation on both sides will enable advertisers to home in on a vendor's niche in the market," Wise said.

When that happens, mobile budgets will follow, she said.

"Once an advertiser picks the right vendor that can optimize to their requirements, their campaigns will perform better and they'll be able to justify the spend," Wise said. "Before then, don't throw things at a wall and hope. Do it strategically."

The essentials:

· The most popular formats are **display** (interstitial or banner, dynamic or static, regulated by the IAB & MMA), and **native mobile formats**, such as advertising in the news feed on Facebook (in vogue but not standardized). Native delivers 20 to 60% more engagement than traditional banners.

· **Mobile video ads** are booming. These attract marketers who find a familiar format to television advertising, allowing for rich storytelling. It's advisable to develop video specifically for the mobile.

· The best ads pack the most **impact in a small format**. They are refreshed often and present offers relevant to the mobile user's context.

· **Ad blockers** are a very strong signal for marketers: the public is tired of intrusive ads. Creativity is improving, and the ability to deliver targeted messages, at the right time, is being perfected.

· Ad servers, partners, and publishers must be able to rotate different versions of visuals, whatever they are. Performance reports are required to compare click-through rates, conversion rates, and ultimately ROI. Always make **quick, decisive changes**.

· Use **targeting data** wisely. Prefer primary data versus derived data. Advances in "big data" data analysis allow for increasingly sophisticated customization scenarios.

· In a world where cookies are unreliable, the marketer's basic tool is a good tool for **tracking and attributing** downloads. Two categories of features are covered: analysis of user behaviors and optimization, or testing of different versions.

PART 3

MONETIZATION: EARNING PROFITS FROM TRAFFIC

The publisher's main priority is building an application that will be enjoyed and used. To do so, the focus must be on the product first, and monetization second. We have already discussed that new applications do not thrive only on the basis of word-of-mouth, and that marketing, while expensive and requiring resources to execute, is necessary for any app that wants to stand out. The application developer is therefore constantly searching for sources of revenue, and for many applications, a main source is advertising. This section explores the possibilities of using advertising to generate income. You will recall that the vast majority of successful applications are free, and rely on a freemium and/or advertising model to make money. Here, we will explore the different ways of using advertising for these purposes, whether the app sells something, or relies solely on advertising.

CHAPTER 8
DEFINING A STRATEGY AND MAXIMIZING YIELD

Executive summary

The freemium model forces publishers to master advertising monetization tools.

A good advertising strategy increases both revenue and loyalty.

A good understanding of **technology**, but also of the **motivations** of the ecosystem's actors is necessary for success.

Defining a strategy: understanding business models and selection criteria

CASE STUDY

THE IMPORTANCE OF ADVERTISING FOR ZYNGA

The game publisher Zynga has in recent years begun to follow the migration of its audience from social network games to mobile games. Historically, it derived most of its revenues from the sale of products in free games (in-app purchases). The migration towards mobile has forced Zynga to reinvent monetization and increase its reliance on advertising. In 2011, ad sales represented $74 million, or 7% of revenues. In 2015, that more than doubled to $173 million, or 23% of revenues. About 75% of this revenue comes from mobile.

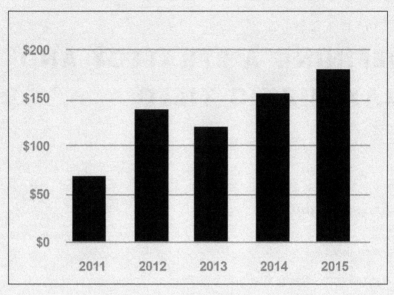

Figure 8.1 – Zynga's advertising revenues, millions of dollars

Most publishers will openly say that they developed their application with user experience as a priority. The secret that no one talks about is that applications that earn money have been built with monetization objectives from the start.

Application publishers spend a lot of time balancing user experience and monetization. Some people think that having satisfied users and generating revenues through advertising are mutually exclusive concepts, that ads discourage in-app purchases, irritate users and ultimately drive them out of the application - leaving publishers and advertisers on two opposite sides.

In fact, there is a wealth of data to support the idea that advertising, in native format, video, or rewarded formats, improves several key indicators relevant to publishers and brands, including user LTV. The challenge is to understand that the interests of brands and publishers are in fact very compatible. Their shared risk of irritating consumers must be overcome by a mutually beneficial advertising solution. LTV is the result of a three-part equation: monetization (revenues from advertisements, subscriptions or purchases in the application), retention (largely based on the engagement and lifetime of the user) and virality (the value of each user referring others).

From the brand's point of view, the advertiser is interested in maximizing the consumer's engagement with advertising, presenting their brand in the best way, and leaving a favorable impression that will lead to a subsequent purchase. These objectives are fully aligned with those of the publisher. Neither the brand nor the publisher benefit from horrifying the user with intrusive, badly targeted and untimely ads!

EXAMPLE

One of Cheetah Mobile's customers, the publisher of a popular free calendar application, wanted to improve user experience while increasing LTV by providing relevant content to engage and monetize users. To meet the need, Cheetah Mobile created a simple advertising format: a native advertisement on the app's lock screen. The revenue from this application tripled to millions per month, with a 20% increase in active daily users, and an increase in the total number users to over 100 million[1].

In another case, FusePowered examined native rewarded videos and found that not only are these ads not an obstacle to in-app purchases (IAPs), they improve the number of IAPs and their mean value: "Of those who do not watch a rewarded video, only 0.7% have made an IAP. In comparison, 4.7% of players who watched a rewarded video made an IAP. The players who watched the rewarded video were six times likelier to convert than those who did not.[2]"

This demonstrates that a well-thought-out advertising strategy can contribute to sustainable revenue generation for publishers.

HOW DOES IT WORK?

To insert ads into their app, developers need to sign up with an ad network, install the SDK, or HTML or JavaScript link, and choose the location of the ads. For each ad network, there are rules that specify what types of applications are permitted to display ads and where ads can be displayed (this is to ensure network quality). App developers earn money when users see ads or click on them. These publishers are paid at a cost-per-click (CPC), cost per 1,000 im-

1 Cheetah Mobile, 2016
2 FusePowered (June 2015)

pressions (CPM) or other variants, such as cost per installation basis. A portion of revenue is collected based on the amount the advertiser is willing to pay per click, impression or installation, minus the ad network commission.

WHAT FORMAT?

The decisive factor in the success of monetization is the type (see section on advertising formats) and the positioning of the ads. It's strongly recommended that you start by applying best practices, and iterate immediately by testing variants to find the optimum long-term revenue: the best retention with the best advertising revenue per user (see section on the calculation of the LTV).

Ideally, the advertising formats and timing of delivery work perfectly from the point of view of the user's experience. Is the mobile user reading an article? Use a banner at the top of the page and one at the bottom, and one or two native ads inside the article. Watching a video? Think about putting an ad in the trailer. Stuck on level 5 of your game? Offer an extra life in exchange for watching a promotional video. In general, avoid bombarding the user with interstitial ads as soon as your app or mobile site is opened. Always wait for the user to have engaged with several screens before displaying an interstitial ad. The CPM of an early ad will be good, but the likelihood of losing the user is high. As a result, you'll forfeit other revenue opportunities.

Figure 8.2 - Banner and interstitial ads

PUBLISHER TIPS ON VIEWABILITY

Clearly express formats specifications to advertisers, ad exchanges, agencies and other partners. This will save you from going back and forth trying to understand why a campaign does not deliver impressions. Additionally, if some of them are unusual formats (for example, vertical video), use an ad server that can either "transform" the visual and adapt it to your format, or completely prevent it from being displayed if it's not the right format. Nothing is more irritating for the mobile user than to receive an error message on an advertising placement.

More and more advertisers, especially brands and their agencies, place great importance on the ability to measure the true viewability of an advertisement (see the available tools in the previous chapter). Indeed, your mobile site can appear differently in portrait or landscape format, and from one smartphone to another (screen sizes vary, etc.). It is a good idea to test the appearance of advertising spaces on as many devices as possible.

Best practices vary from one application category to another. The publisher will do well to carry out a complete competitive analysis.

EXAMPLE

A content-rich application (such as a mobile game review app) may create a short section at the end of each article recommending similar applications (Figure 8.3), and/or a separate section listing applications to download. This latter format (Figure 8.4), commonly called an "app wall", is very popular and may include rewards for installing a promoted app. We shall see later how to optimize the order of displayed applications.

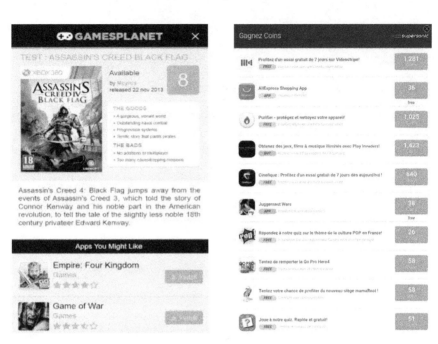

Figure 8.3 - Recommendations section   **Figure 8.4 – App wall**

Interstitial formats deliver captivating full-screen ads during breaks in the app. They allow advertisers to convey their message in large format and often generate attractive returns. This is why CPMs for interstitial ads are generally higher than those for standard banners. An intelligent banner will reorient itself and change its size dynamically when the user turns their smartphone in order to preserve the quality of the brand experience.

Let's not forget mobile websites. With a completely different design from both applications and their computer counterparts, they require a dedicated approach. The most harmonious formats will be banners or videos inserted in the content ("in-stream"), as well as the creation of recommendation sections. You can also cautiously use interstitials when the user navigates from one article to another. You should avoid very small, or vertical, banner formats (not enough space), as well as advertising links (too small). Low yields will be expected from the top and bottom banner, which will often be ignored, but may be useful for brands looking for exposure at a low price –favor brands, not performance-based advertisers, in these placements.

< FOCUS >

UNDERSTANDING THE MECHANISMS OF REWARDED ADVERTISING

Mobile video ad formats are growing rapidly, especially in mobile games. In particular, the rewarded video format is becoming more and more popular, and there are many advertising platforms offering rewarded video solutions (such as Fyber, Vungle, NativeX, Tapjoy, etc.). Remember that this format involves an "exchange of value" between the user, who accepts to watch a video advertisement, and the publisher, who in return offers a free advantage in the application (e.g. some in-game currency, or a free life). Finally, the ad platform pays the publisher if the user decides to download the advertised application. This three-player model has economic repercussions that need to be considered.

The publishers give the reward out when the video ad is displayed. From their point of view, this reward is given to the user instead of selling it for cash. For example, a game can credit the user with 5 gems in exchange for watching a video ad. The affiliate network's SDK usually provides a signal that allows the developer to know that the view of the video is completed so that the developer can unlock the reward.

However, the publisher is not paid at the time the reward is distributed. Most video affiliate networks do not pay for the viewing of a video. They instead pay a share of the income they receive. Being paid on a performance basis means that the publisher is paid for the number of downloads that these video advertisements may have generated. If the video is interesting and if the user likes the app, he downloads, installs and opens it. Only then will the publisher will be paid.

To evaluate whether reward based advertising is worth it, the publisher must compare the potential shortfall (would this user have bought the 5 gemstones anyway?), with the advertising revenue. Unfortunately, affiliate network performance reports do not offer precise data at the individual user's level, making this comparison almost impossible. The marketer is limited to using approximations and averages.

Finally, some publishers can afford to create unique advertising formats. Pandora, for example, offers audio spots. To do this, you need to have a large enough audience that advertisers can justify creating specific content for your support (which you can facilitate by providing free creative services), and a direct sales force that will be able to explain the format to advertisers and their agencies. It's not for everyone.

CONSUMER PROTECTION

In addition to the selection of formats, I recommend that the publisher pays particular attention to the ease with which the user can close the ad and unsubscribe from targeting. For static interstitial formats, the closing icon must be very visible. It is necessary to monitor its color and size, and to check that it is visible on all types of backgrounds. For a trailer or interstitial video, the option to stop must appear quickly enough to find the right balance between a satisfactory viewability for the advertiser and less inconvenience for the user who wants to continue on their way. Consider the example of TrueView, the skippable video ad format for apps recently launched by Google's AdMob. With this format, a developer can choose where in his application the user will see the video ad (i.e. a natural pause in the game, for example between two levels). The user watches the first five seconds of the ad, then a button is displayed that allows the user to close the ad and return to where they were. The format works well: the user only views what they want, the advertiser is satisfied that the user viewed the ad because they were interested, and the developer receives significant revenue, while providing a less annoying experience to the user.

An aside: always ensure that advertising can be clearly identified as such. A mention such as "Presented by," "Sponsored by," "Advertisement," or "Paid Advertising" may be relevant.

The "AdChoices" icon is used in the United States and Europe to allow the user to unsubscribe from specific targeting. Similarly, Apple and Android offer the option to unsubscribe from physical or behavioral tracking (this does not disable advertising, just targeting). Publishers in the United States must pay close attention to the FTC's rules regarding advertising. In December 2015, the organization released a new policy to reinforce their views on native advertising, warning the industry that publishers have no right to make mobile users believe that native ads are editorial content. Care must be taken to respect the consumer protection laws in the countries where you will be advertising. For example, European law mandates to inform consumers about the use of advertising cookies, and requires the prior consent of the consumer before using personal data for behavioral targeting purposes.

It is now common knowledge that ad blocking software has wind in its sails. Although is still restricted on mobile, some publishers have reacted violently to their introduction, going from blaming mobile users, all the way to blocking content for ad-blocker users. A much better strategy consists of taking advantage of this opportunity to listen to users' needs and improve their experience. Moreover, most of these programs offer a white list of publishers eligible to show ads that meet certain criteria. These "acceptable ads" are often defined as non-animated, clearly-labeled, and non-disruptive. That being said, it is important to know that ad-blockers do not have the technical capacity to automatically recognize ads that meet their selection criteria. The publisher will therefore need to contact the ad-blocker and demonstrate compliance to be included on their white list.

FACT SHEET

PUBLISHER TIPS FOR NATIVE ADVERTISING

Unlike banners, where ads are updated every 30-60 seconds, native ads need a more persistent presence. When they appear in the news feed, which can be used in a fast scroll mode, it is important to give the user a chance to go back to an ad.

As a result, refresh rates for native ads on social, information and m-commerce apps may be limited to 1-2 minutes or even once per session - depending on the average length of the sessions.

IS A SALES TEAM REQUIRED?

We saw earlier that native formats performed best for advertisers and users. Predictably, they also generate the best revenue for publishers. They also provide better control of user experience and demonstrate creativity. However, we know that native formats are still not very prevalent in the industry, and as a result, the publisher can expect an incomplete fill rate. On the other hand, standard IAB formats are heavily used by advertisers, especially DSPs, but offer CPMs that can be quite low. What shall a publisher do?

The main issue is achieving a balance between a high CPM and a high fill rate. Indeed, many ad networks can promise a very high CPM. But how many impressions will they be able to buy at this price? Often, the best CPMs are obtained for highly restrictive targeting, or limited ad formats. Moreover, the publisher is generally able to obtain better prices by selling his inventory himself, because he is better able to pitch it. However, most publishers do not have the sales force necessary to sell all of their impressions - or even to sell a portion of them. Here's how the math works: for example, a great application receives 100,000 active visitors per day, each of which is exposed to 3 ads. That's 300,000 impressions for sale per day. At an average price of $1 CPM, the revenue will be $300 per day. How many campaigns will it take to sell these impressions? Will it be possible to pay a salesperson's salary with this revenue? How about someone to manage the campaigns? What's the incremental difficulty of getting the last dollar? Only about a hundred applications worldwide have enough traffic to justify having a direct sales team. If that's your case, bravo! If not, it doesn't matter. There's a whole market dedicated to helping you sell your inventory.

It is therefore recommended, and even necessary, to work with several suppliers and in several formats. We will see later how to allocate the inventory to each type of need.

HOW TO CHOOSE AN ADVERTISING PARTNER?

There are myriads of affiliate networks and DSPs. It's not realistic to test them all. To sort through them, start by asking the right questions, and consult the various forums to verify their reputation. The blog Soomla has a comparison table with some of the basic information[3]. Here are the main criteria to look for:

- Payment:
  - Model (CPC, CPM, CPI)
  - Percentage shared with the publisher
  - Terms (when is the publisher paid)
  - Payment conditions (and conditions of refusal of payment)
  - Payment methods (PayPal, bank transfer, check, etc.)

- Offer:
  - Quality of the offers
  - Relevancy of the offers for your audience
  - Quantity of offers and budget sizes
  - Direct relationship with the advertiser (to get the best prices and biggest budgets)

- Formats

- International presence

- Dedicated account management and operational support:
  - In a language and time zone that suits you
  - Transparency of your inventory to the advertiser (desirable or not, according to your direct sales strategy)

- Technology:
  - Reliability
  - Flexibility of integration options (preference for those that offer at least two possibilities between tag, API and SDK).
  - Technical support

- Performance:
  - Efficiency of the offer and creative optimization algorithm
  - Access to a large source of proprietary data for better targeting Integration with DMPs

---

3 Soomla (May 2016), *Mobile Ad Networks Comparison Spreadsheet*

WHICH PAYMENT MODEL?

There is a common perception that brand campaigns are better paying for publishers and better perceived by users. Let's dismantle this myth:

The publisher's total revenue is equal to average CPM times fill rate. Brand campaigns often offer high CPMs. In exchange, they select the best impressions, and only the best impressions, and the best inventory (because the brand pays to be placed prominently). Not all ad placements are the best, not all users are the best, and you're unlikely to find a portfolio of brands with perfectly complementary requirements. The publisher is therefore likely to end up with unsold inventory. Who is interested by it?

Performance advertisers desire to acquire the right users at the right price. They are therefore generally open to the idea of being placed in many advertising formats, and presented to many kinds of users. Performance advertisers are good candidates to buy unsold inventory. When they pay on a CPC, CPI, CPA, or some other basis, publishers share the risk, having no CPM guarantee - but they can calculate an eCPM ("effective CPM") after the fact, to compare campaigns.

The advent of sales in a programmatic way eliminates these differences: in an RTB system, all advertisers pay on a CPM basis. The CPM is not guaranteed and varies based on the estimated inventory value, which in theory allows performance based advertisers to pay more than brands for users who they consider having a high probability of delivering a good LTV. For the publisher, in theory, the RTB system should maximize the revenue of each impression. We will explore this in a specific chapter.

< FOCUS >

LET'S BE REALISTIC: WHAT'S THE VALUE OF MY INVENTORY?

The CPM, or eCPM, that a publisher can expect varies enormously. In general, it will be lower for mobile sites than for applications (the latter being favored by advertisers for their traceability, and the former having a significant share of inventory with less efficient formats and placements). A productivity application (e.g. an antivirus) will have a lower eCPM because its users will be less engaged in it than an entertainment application (e.g. Spotify). An e-mail application, in which users are not in "shopping mode", will get lower eCPMs than a m-commerce or photo sharing app, such as Pinterest. A gambling application, attracting a very specific and lucrative target, will get double-digit CPMs.

Ad format also has an enormous influence on price. A rewarded video format will bring in close to $20 CPM. However, publishers will have to limit it to a few impressions per day, per user, or risk alienating users and decreasing advertiser ROI. An exclusive, or unique, format, such as a native format dedicated to a brand (for example the creation of a custom filter on Snapchat during an event such as the Oscars) can easily cost over $750,000.

WHAT ARE THE TECHNICAL NEEDS?

To display advertising, it will be necessary to encode placements and formats in the mobile site, or application. To do this, publishers can use an ad server, a partner, a mediation tool, or some combination of these options. The code will include visual elements (banner, video, call-to-action, logo, etc.), target landing page (App Store, mobile web site or deep link), tracking and verification technologies, audience targeting parameters, and campaign conditions (price, maximum frequency, daily budget, etc.). Three types of codes exist, each with its advantages and disadvantages, which will be an integral part of your choice criteria:

- Tag (HTML / JavaScript): calls the ad server (either yours or your partner's) to download the ad each time the page downloads.
  - Advantages: versatile and easy to implement, it is often a good way to start. It supports dynamic formats (through JavaScript). It works for mobile websites and applications. It allows the tracking and counting of impressions.
  - Disadvantages: must be implemented placement by placement, and partner by partner. Does not lend itself to easy optimization between different sources of offers, nor to large scale expansion: the tag must be changed for each new campaign. If the campaign has run out of daily budget (cap), the ad cannot be switched dynamically (at best, it can redirect to a static back-fill campaign).
- "API" (application programming interface): the process by which advertisement offers are received automatically, as a group. It can be synchronous or asynchronous.

- Advantages: in asynchronous use, allows for obtaining all available offers in advance (say, once per day), decide on an optimal order of presentation, and cache ads inside the website or app for a faster download. This productivity gain is also a gain of efficiency, because it allows for testing more offers, and optimizing them in a quicker manner. In synchronous use, APIs allow real-time rotation of offers, for example to only show offers that still have available daily budget at 5 p.m.. The MRAID IAB standard is a synchronous API.
- Disadvantages: asynchronous APIs are not compatible with tracking and verification technologies desired by brands and agencies. Additionally, they do not enable advertisers to use their preferred ad servers. They are therefore better suited for performance based campaigns. Synchronous API eliminate some of these deficits but do not cache ads. As a result, they do not improve ads downloading speed. Furthermore, neither API type can leverage publisher-specific proprietary data for targeting.

- Software Development Kit (SDK): a code that must be integrated within the application (available only for applications and not for mobile websites), and that manages the targeting, presentation, selection and tracking of advertisements. A publisher can integrate multiple SDKs within the same application.
  - Advantages: the king of advertising technology on apps. Allows total flexibility in terms of ad formats, monitoring, viewability and ad serving tools (as long as they are included in the SDK), and allows user ID to be used in real time for targeting purposes. This makes it the preferred tool for networks.
  - Disadvantages: weight is a major problem. To ensure good app responsiveness and user experience, especially on a 3G network, the publisher is limited to integrating no more than two or three SDKs. Given that the developers probably already implemented one or two SDKs for the analysis and optimization of the app, this does not leave the marketer much room to add monetization SDKs. In addition, quite a few SDKs will collect information about users (such as their geographic location) that will be used for targeting. As a result, the question of data ownership arises: the SDK enables its owner to create user databases, and earn money at the publisher's expense. As a result of these two factors, most publishers will, in practice, gravitate towards implementing a very small number of SDKs, from major advertising platforms.

SUMMARY OF MOBILE AD SERVER SELECTION CRITERIA - BY SMART AD SERVER

Smart AdServer is an ad server for publishers who want to offer a premium advertising experience. Here are their recommendations:

- Formats:
  - Diversity of the advertising formats (in-stream video, pre-roll, native, rich media, etc.).
  - Rapid innovation to integrate the new buzz formats (such as vertical video, Snapchat's flagship format).
  - Flexibility in creating proprietary formats.
  - Possibility of visualizing the rendering of the creatives from a mobile test application.

- Advanced targeting capabilities:
  - OS, screen size, hardware, etc.
  - Proprietary data management.
  - Connection to DMPs to access third-party data.

- Analyses:
  - Capabilities and quality of the analysis interfaces and reports.
  - Inventory forecast.

- Standards support:
  - MRAID (rich media visuals), VAST and VPAID for video.
  - IAB Mobile certification.
  - Compatible with Google AMP and Facebook Instant Articles.

- Certification and integration with agencies' preferred technologies:
  - Standard ad servers, such as Double Click or Atlas.
  - Verification and certification technologies (Moat, Integral Ad Science, etc.).
- Simplicity of campaign programming: unified management of platforms and screens (iOS/Android, screen sizes)
  - Ad server compatibility with mobile websites and apps.

Despite its techy exterior, digital advertising requires many manual steps. Each tool and partner that's been mentioned must be managed. Publishers must decide on formats and publishing rules, monitor their application, sign purchase orders, prioritize orders, monitor fill rates and average daily eCPM, allocate inventory to campaigns, and so on.

Mediation

Mediation enables an application developer to optimize the number and sequence of ads in an app, to maximize yield.

Firstly, the fill rate, which is the percentage of ad requests met by the diffusion of an ad, is one of the most important statistics that an application developer needs to monitor. Ideally, the developer's fill rate should be 100%, which means that an ad is diffused to a user each time an impression is generated. Even if payment is on a click or install basis, the more users see ads, the more likely they are to click on them, thereby increasing your revenue. However, few ad networks can provide a 100% fill rate to application developers. Often, they don't have enough offers that correspond precisely to the supply. In other words, ad networks do not have enough advertisers who promote diverse advertising campaigns (or spend enough) to always have an ad to show for each of the impressions that an app generates. To increase the offer fill rate at once, a publisher needs to use ad mediation, which enables them to show ads coming from multiple ad networks. There are several mediation services. The two main ones are Google, with AdMob, and Twitter, with MoPub.

The order in which inventory is offered to advertising partners determines the price at which each impression is sold. Let's take for example a publisher who has 10 million impressions to sell, and non-guaranteed IOs with Coca-Cola and Louis Vuitton. There are two possible ways of allocating the inventory, of which one generates almost twice the revenue of the other:

Advertiser	Budget	CPM	Desired impressions	Sequentially allocated impressions	Impressions allocated to maximize the eCPM
1 - Coca-Cola	$10,000	$1	10,000,000	10,000,000	9,000,000
2 - LouisVuitton	$10,000	$10	1,000,000	0	1,000,000
	Publisher revenue			$10,000	$19,000

Table 8.1 - Financial impact of the impression allocation order

In order for this to work, the publisher needs to configure ad mediation for the app, add the ad networks' SDKs, and assign them a priority order. Logically, the publisher should start with the network offering the highest CPM, then continue with the next, and so on.

The ad mediation's yield optimization feature evaluates the CPM of each network in the mediation stack and reorganizes these networks dynamically. Thus, it is the network with the highest CPM at any time that is diffusing an ad in the app.

FACT SHEET

WHICH MEDIATION PLATFORM TO CHOOSE?

There are many mediation services. I recommend focusing on mobile specialists. The biggest are Twitter ("MoPub" platform), Google ("AdMob" platform) and Rubicon. The main selection criteria are:

- Number and variety of connections to ad sources:
  - Affiliate networks
  - Ad exchanges
  - Direct offers
- Complexity and flexibility of the prioritization algorithm:
  - Possibility of automatic optimization
  - Possibility to decide the criteria manually
  - Integration of RTB - especially, are all impressions included in RTB or only those that remain after priority networks have made their choice?

- Programmatic and monetization features:
  - Ability to send all the data to programmatic buyers (unique identifiers, application names, connection type, etc.)
  - Multiple connections with the main mobile DSPs;
  - Management of all programmatic or non-programmatic purchasing methods (RTB, reserved IOs, guaranteed programmatic, etc.)
  - Ability to deliver rich media, native and video in a programmatic way;
  - Mediation and compatibility with Facebook Audience Network.

- Complexity of the technical integration and inventory management

- Simplicity in integrating the statistics required for decision-making: is it possible to dynamically integrate the revenue reports generated by the networks, so that eCPM calculation is automatic?

In general, mediation is free for publishers, as most mediation platforms are also mobile advertising platforms and thus paid for by advertisers. It is in their financial interest to increase the number of publishers to which they can connect these advertisers to, in order to grow advertising budgets. This conflict of interest can be a concern for a publisher. Indeed, if a mediation platform is in charge of optimizing the rank of advertisers, how can you be sure that it will not prioritize its own? Few publishers truly understand the prioritization mechanisms used by their mediation platform. Moreover, as a move towards a lucrative niche, and to seduce publishers with a full suite of services, many affiliate networks now offer mediation solutions. The SSP platforms do this as well, and, as if it was not already complicated enough, affiliate networks are launching RTB programs. The lids of these "black boxes" must be lifted and the partners' fundamental motivations understood. A partner that is a pure technological solution, without conflict of interest, is your best bet.

The waterfall model

Having integrated myriads of affiliate networks, participated in ad exchanges in RTB, and managed to sell a few direct campaigns, the successful publisher finds himself faced with a complex puzzle when allocating inventory. A simplified example:

Campaign	Payment method	Price	Budget	Guarantee?	eCPM	Ideal position
Louis Vuitton	CPM	$10	$10,000	No	$10	2
Coca-Cola	CPM	$1	$10,000	Yes	$1	1
Candy Crush	CPI	$1.50	$100,000	No	$3	3
Rewarded video network	CPI	Varies	$25,000	No	$20	4
Display network	CPC	Varies	$5,000	No	$0.20	6
RTB	CPM	Varies	$5,000	No	$0.50	5

Table 8.2 – Example of inventory allocation to maximize yield[4]

In this case, it would make sense to prioritize direct campaigns (Coca-Cola, Louis Vuitton and Candy Crush). Indeed, for strategic reasons, it is essential to deliver the full allocated budget: most advertisers can rapidly increase budget, or launch new campaigns, for high-performing publishers. Many agencies allocate a test budget at the beginning of the month, and decide after a week or two to which publishers to further allocate budget, depending on their ability to deliver traffic. In addition, direct advertisers are generally brands that offer a publisher-controlled advertising experience, acceptable to the user. They are therefore to be favored from a long-term perspective, even if short term revenue is suboptimal.

Among direct campaigns, which should receive priority? First, the commercial obligations must be fulfilled and the guaranteed campaigns must be delivered. In this case, Coca-Cola will have bought a delivery guarantee of its entire budget, to the detriment of Louis Vuitton if there are not enough impressions to satisfy the latter's budget. Care should be taken by publishers in the matter of inventory guarantee clauses - the price must be worth it.

Then, among direct campaigns, favor those with the strongest eCPM. Here, the algorithm can base its calculation on historical data to calculate that the Louis Vuitton campaign, with a CPM of $10, must be delivered before that of Candy Crush, with an eCPM of $3.

---

4 To be calculated based on historical performance data, or estimates, absent past information

For indirect campaigns, the algorithm (provided that it is fed with recent and correct data), will be able to prioritize according to eCPM and remaining budget. It should be noted that the rewarded format, despite its strong eCPM compared to direct campaigns, is correctly placed in position 4. It is a format to be used sparingly. Another way to limit its effect is to apply a maximum frequency to that network (frequency cap).

And so it goes, until all budgets, or all available impressions, have been exhausted – whichever comes first. If there are any leftover impressions, the publisher has to decide the behavior of the mediation platform and/or the ad server: don't show advertising at all to protect the mobile user's experience, or show an ad for another of the publisher's applications, or for a paid functionality of the app (both known as "house ads") to reinforce cross-selling and up-selling.

As we have seen above, it is important not to leave complete freedom to the mediation platform, but to decide the general order of priority (or cascade) and let the algorithm optimize within those parameters.

< FOCUS >

AD SERVER, MEDIATION, SSP - UNTANGLING LINGO WITH ONE EXAMPLE

Let us take the example of a news application, such as Flipboard (fictitious situation). Flipboard has direct agreements with some advertisers for which it will use an ad server. A typical scenario would be that Flipboard signs an agreement with Nike and Flipboard's ad server allocates inventory to Nike advertisements. Once Flipboard's salespeople have sold all the inventory they could, there may still be available impressions. This unsold inventory can be monetized, even at a lower CPM, in an ad exchange. Flipboard will then use an SSP to make these impressions available in RTB. In addition, Flipboard may decide to partner with a mobile video ad network to increase its video advertising inventory. A mediation platform will be used to prioritize various ad networks, DSPs, and direct offers. Flipboard, as a publisher, will therefore use all 3 technologies.

The essentials

· **The type and placement of advertising formats** are the key elements that influence monetization and user experience. Preferred formats are IAB interstitial and native. Good formats are good for the consumer too.

· Campaigns can be **procured directly and/or through partnerships**. These are often necessary; the selection and management of partners are key steps.

· **The yield depends on the eCPM and fill rate**. The former is driven by the payment mode (CPM, CPC, CPI, etc.), performance, and type of advertisers. The latter by the number of advertisers and their budgets.

· Two technological building blocks are essential: an **ad server** to display advertisements, and a **mediation layer** to optimize the display order of the campaigns.

· It is important to understand the mediation layer's **prioritization** mechanisms, their possible **biases**, and to parameter behavior preferences. Define a set of principles from which the mediation platform can optimize automatically.

CHAPTER 9

PROGRAMMATIC SELLING AND STUMBLING BLOCKS

Executive summary

Programmatic may have delivered disappointing results to publishers, due to low CPMs and low fill rates, and challenges understanding this complex technology.

Programmatic is a nascent and rapidly growing field that will improve and get closer to the panacea it could be for publishers.

The savvy publisher will navigate around stumbling blocks that reduce yield.

The growth of programmatic advertising is not up for debate. However, this topic is complex and its implementation brings about pitfalls for publishers. Programmatic has been disappointing many publishers, who expected it to perfect and automate yield management, yet find themselves with disappointing eCPM and fill rates. While the industry is in its infancy, both technological advances and the growth of budgets allocated to mobile programmatic (especially those of brands) will improve things. In the meantime, we will look at some RTB concepts that are specific to the publisher, and some strategies to increase the chances of success.

An SSP (Supply Side Platform) is a tool that allows publishers to access advertisers' offers in ad exchanges through real-time bidding. Each impression is auctioned, accompanied by descriptive information, such as its origin (application or mobile site), its placement, its format, its unique identifier (IDFA or GAID), and any of the user information that the publisher wants to share: for example, the user's location, telephone number, or even gender and age. The advertiser views this data, compares it to their intended target audience, and decides on a price to offer. The auction winner gets to display their advertisement to the mobile user.

This mechanism already presents a pitfall for the publisher: all advertisers get access to the shared data, whether they buy the impression, or not. An unscrupulous (or very profit-driven) DSP may submit very low fictitious bid for the sole purpose of collecting information and building rich user profiles, which they can then apply elsewhere. In fact, many publishers choose not to share their critical user data in open RTB systems, instead reserving them for guaranteed buyers with whom they establish direct programmatic contracts. This flaw in the system limits the ability of bidders to offer the best possible price, because many of them are basing their decision on limited and undifferentiated information.

We have seen previously that the quantity of offers available in ad exchanges is limited by the inventory match between formats supplied by publishers, and formats desired by advertisers. Prices and diversity are limited by the number of advertisers - particularly the number of brands - that are generally willing to pay a higher price for select impressions. These factors are related to the novelty of the medium. More fundamentally though, the RTB mechanism tends to push prices down.

Strategically, it will be important to program the mediation platform to reflect the minimum price of your inventory: the floor price. What is the minimum price below which displaying an advertisement no longer makes sense? For example, one can argue that risking alienating the user with one more advertisement for the opportunity to earn another 5 cents CPM is probably not worth it. The question is: what's this minimum? It can't be estimated in an exact mathematical manner, for it would be necessary to take into account the probability that this advertisement and only this advertisement is the drop of water that makes the vase overflow and causes the loss of a mobile user, word-of-mouth opportunity, or another potential shortfall. Without knowing the content of the advertisement in advance, nor the precise reaction of the mobile user (which varies for each person), it is impossible to model it. It will therefore be necessary to decide minimum price in a subjective way and test its impact. The other reason for presenting a minimum price is that, in RTB, it can make the inventory appear as "premium". Indeed, there are a good number of advertisers who use RTB to buy unsold inventory at low prices. If many of these bargain hunters are seduced by a low (or inexistent) floor price, the average eCPM of the application will go down. Its other performance indicators, such as CTR and CVR, can also be impacted, as these advertisements are typically less qualitative. A new brand advertiser, offering a higher CPM, will potentially be discouraged by these metrics, and will skip your inventory, limiting you to low-cost ads. Conversely, publishers have observed a virtuous cycle: if the floor price is raised, average eCPM goes up (fill rate is affected, of course). So what is the ideal floor price? In practice, setting it between 50 and 80% of the desired average eCPM is a good starting point. Consider setting a floor price by geographical area and type of placement.

SOPHISTICATION IN FLOOR PRICES

A publisher (or his SSP) can set either a soft floor price, or a hard floor price. A hard floor price is the minimum price that publishers can tolerate. This basically means that they will not take any offer below that price. A soft floor price acts like a kind of phantom bid that serves to inflate prices. This threshold captures what can be considered as missed opportunities when buyers bid a little below the desired price. How does it work?

- **Hard floor price**: The highest bid wins, and pays the price of the second highest bid.

- **Soft floor price**: If all offers are higher than the soft floor price, the price paid by the winning bid (always the highest bid) is the price of the second highest bid. If all offers are lower than the soft floor price, the price paid by the winning bid (always the highest bid) will be the price offered (i.e. the highest bid price).

An illustrative example:

	Without soft floor price	With soft floor price
Hard floor price	$1	$1
Soft floor price		$5
Bid A	$2	$2
Bid B	$1.50	$1.50
Price paid by winning auction (A)	$1.50	$2

Table 9.1 - The soft floor price

This represents an artificial price increase of 33% for the buyer. Besides the sense-lessness of short-circuiting a dynamic market place with artificial prices, this practice can be seen as dishonest by advertisers, who are equipped with software that detects soft floor prices and can fictitiously bid to determine where the real (hard) floor price is. This algorithmic war between advertisers and publishers is a waste of time for everyone and does not benefit the world of advertising.

Transparency is a solution. Direct relationships between advertisers and publishers (through the creation of direct programmatic contracts, whether they are guaranteed or not) allow publishers to obtain a fair value for their inventory, and advertisers to have confidence in the paid price.

Another possible solution is the use of a dynamic floor price, available on some SSPs. The RTB system allows the sophisticated publisher to collect a lot of nuanced information on the market. The highest bid wins, but other bids are not really lost because they can be analyzed by the SSP. This information on the dynamics of the market (what was the second bid, the third, how many advertisers placed bids?) allows for establishing a future price by simulating a fictitious auction: the SSP algorithm simulates bids in a price range and calculates the result that would have been obtained, based on the tested floor price. During the simulation, the system records the revenue earned for each impression in a plethora of scenarios. After the simulation is done, another algorithm calculates the revenue at each tested floor price and determines at what floor price revenue is maximized. These simulations can be performed on each segment of inventory where the publisher uses a dynamic floor.

Proprietary data: the goose that lays golden eggs?

There was a time when publishers were satisfied with general representations of their audience to sell their inventory to advertisers and agencies. We referred to demographic groups (this application is used by young men aged 15 to 25) and behavioral preferences (who love motorcycles and travel). These analyses of the audience could be carried out periodically using questionnaires or cross-referencing. Today, advertisers and agencies expect each impression to be qualified by demographic and behavioral data about each specific user. In our previous example, knowing that 80% of an app's audience is male is not enough, now the advertiser wants to distinguish that a specific impression is from a female mobile user, in real time. Blessed is the publisher who is in possession of this information – they will be able to monetize it at a higher CPM price, or even to resell it to DMPs who'll add it to user profiles.

One of the most frequent and valuable data points is the user's physical location (via GPS, or beacon, for example) but it requires permission to get collected. As much as obtaining permission makes sense for a navigation application, asking for it in a gaming application is not justifiable and will probably incite mistrust from users, resulting in uninstalls. Some services, such as The Wireless Registry, propose to implement their SDK in apps to collect users' positional data over time and create profiles for resale purposes. For example, all users of a mobile game that regularly attend a golf course will be classified as golfers, enabling the publisher to increase the price of their impressions. If this option is chosen, it should be implemented with serious and transparent partners, who will protect users' privacy.

Kudos to publishers who leverage an intimate understanding of the user path to collect data at the right time. For example, you should not ask a new user of a clothing sales app what style she prefers on the first visit. On the other hand, at the end of the third visit, it makes sense to offer to improve recommendations based on a short questionnaire. Little by little, by combining responses with in-app behaviors, you can draw up a precise profile of this user.

Ads and app monetization – three things you're still doing wrong!

Missed monetization opportunities come down to what publishers are not doing. Publishers are often unaware that highly-converting monetization moments come from identifying when a user is completing organic or utility-based actions.

Other revenue missteps come from not properly planning for the complexities of scaling and internationalization.

Here are 3 monetization pitfalls for publishers to avoid, and ideas on how to turn them around if you may have already fallen.

1. You're relying on programmatic RTB too much

RTB programmatic for publishers was supposed to be the end-all and be-all of in-app advertising. The theory was that by selling via programmatic in a transparent system, publishers could build relationships with advertisers, earn greater CPMs and have control over ad placements, thereby ensuring user satisfaction and lifetime value. From the advertiser's perspective, this was great because (supposedly) RTB makes it easy for buyers to pick and choose the highest returning impressions.

But the feedback that I am hearing from many publishers about RTB is that they are either seeing high eCPMs with poor fill rates, or if they set their floor price too low they get low eCPMs and high fill rate.

Why? Because advertisers unfortunately don't yet have the right tools and data they need to justify competitive bidding at scale.

Programmatic buying is looked at by advertisers and agencies as a trendy, "must-have" marketing channel to quickly spend budget with hope of high-conversions by using the latest ad tech. Yet most of the time it results in adding limited value. This stems from two big problems with RTB right now:

- There is currently a limited availability of mobile programmatic inventory, making a full-fledged targeting strategy across large media plans less than feasible.

- Publishers lack the proprietary data about their audiences that increases the value of their placements to advertisers.

Eventually, I expect a handful of players to emerge in the RTB space that can enable publishers to leverage their audience, and provide better tools to advertisers to jump into auction-based buying. Until then, RTB should play only a minor role in your overall ad strategy.

2. You're not finding moments of utility

Great native calls to action are found in behavioral moments of utility — catching the engaged user in the act of doing something they do every day and offering a better way to complete the task, or get value, from their effort. In other words, if you want to get my attention, don't make me change my natural behaviors — complement them.

Apps are an important part of our lives. They are with us 24/7 and we rely on them to learn, go, communicate, buy, and share. We are constantly opening, closing, tapping, and swiping our apps. Some of these behaviors can be good opportunities for non-intrusive engagement.

Consider something as simple as a lock screen. Can you believe that on average, people check their phones 150 times a day?! That is a huge number, and a massive amount of engagement. Keep in mind that the 'unlocking' behavior, that takes place when a user is looking at their phone, happens before they even get to their app. It's untouched screen real estate, right there in front of the user, just as they are doing something very natural. Push notifications but also lock screen ads (such as Cheetah Mobile's, as seen above), leverage that space.

Or consider the "saving screen" offered by Hay Day, where is advertiser is the hero enabling the user to reach the next level, even if she failed the current one. Publishers, dive into user paths and imagine advertisements that fit in natural breaks.

3. You never made a scalable plan for international monetization
Most app publishers are (or try to be) global from the get-go. Yet it is challenging to find the best monetization solution in each region as demand sources and preferred ad formats vary significantly. To scale apps globally, you need access to major brands that local consumers can easily identify, trust, respond to and engage with.

Let's imagine you'd like to reach the audience of m-commerce apps. If you're in India, you'd ideally want to advertise in Flipkart. In the Middle East, you'll want to showcase in the likes of Souq. Building and maintaining these relationships is complex and expensive. You need partners on the ground level of each market that you want to enter — each region has brands that local users will consider "premium" you will want to work with to deliver universally higher eCPMs and better fill rates.

This need for local market knowledge and partnerships is especially pronounced in the realm of direct sales. Publishers do direct sales deals to be able to share data with advertisers in a way that's more controlled and ensures a premium inventory. Yet this requires a local sales force. And if you have a local sales force producing in volume, you also need an ad operations team to manage a variety of ad formats and tracking standards. Direct sales can create a lot of very expensive headaches.

Developing the in-house competencies to manage each of these foreign market permeations isn't realistic for most publishers. It's expensive, complex, and distracting. That's why identifying the right partners is vital.

One Last Thought...

Monetizing apps at global scale is difficult. A complex landscape of DSPs and local brands combined with advertiser's delay in adopting emerging sell-side methods are part of the problem. But it is absolutely worth taking the time to get it right.

As a publisher you have other things that are at the core of your business, like turning out great product. Keep your energy and engineers focused there and find a handful of key partners with feet on the ground in global markets to handle the other stuff.

The essentials

· Set a **minimum floor price**. Its calculation can be very complex.

· Regarding formats, think about the **match** between available inventory and popular sizes for advertisers.

· **Proprietary user data** can be highly monetized. A smart strategy is to build up user profiles based on behavior data points gleaned and direct user surveys.

· It is essential to have a limited number of **reliable and specialized partners**, by type of advertising, and by geographical location.

· The best call-to-actions are found in **moments of utility**. To attract attention, one must not attempt to change the mobile user's natural behaviors, but encourage them.

ACKNOWLEDGEMENTS

I would like to start by thanking Eric Dosquet, for suggesting writing this book in the first place. Without him, and had I not been on a streak of saying yes to new ideas, this book would not have seen the light of day. Eric has contributed significant ideas to the book, and many metaphors herein are the result of his fluid prose. Writing a book was not on my bucket list, but, as I did, I discovered a tremendous enjoyment to sharing my passion for elegant marketing. I have Eric to thank for that. Eric is Chief Innovation Officer for France & Benelux at Avanade, a joint venture between Accenture and Microsoft, and co-author of several books on IoT, Mobile marketing and innovation. He is also board member of startups in France, Switzerland and the USA.

Frederic Dosquet also contributed greatly to this work. His findings transpire in the section on marketing theories and consumer behavior mechanics. While I have practiced marketing for 15 years, I have received little formal training on it. Frederic's approach was instrumental in looking for frameworks and concepts, both new and traditional, to explain the *Mobile Native's* behaviors. Frederic is Professor at Pau Business School (France), and a PhD in Marketing. He is the author of 15 marketing books and more than 50 international symposium and academic papers. He also consults for many print, radio and TV media companies.

Scott Valentine, my beloved editor, stands out amongst those that have saved my hide when things threatened to get off-track. He's kept me on pace, and tirelessly reviewed and perfected the copy. I've trusted him to immediately grasp my sometimes very technical meaning and express ideas in my own voice. Scott runs CopyandPR, a great little marketing communications agency specialized in mobile, apps, and Ad Tech. On the design side, John Matthews, of Book Connectors, Lou Strano, of Strano Design, and Andy Harrington, of Bald Guy Interactive, all displayed nerves of steel under stringent deadlines.

A tip of the hat, as well, to the vibrant global mobile marketing community, which generously shared their experiences with me. Notably: Allison Schiff, Senior Editor at AdExchanger, Thomas Bouttefort, Growth & Marketing at

Shapr, Cyril Zimmermann, CEO at HiMedia, the Smart Ad Server team (Marine Desoutter & Ahmed Chakroun), Eli Curetti, CEO at Shopmium, Claire Roederer, Lecturer at University of Strasburg, Gerard Danaguezian, CEO at Moby Survey, Sebastien Megraud, Associate at Media Crossing, Antony Faby, Head of Studio at Gameloft, and Djamel Agaoua, CEO at Viber.

Heartfelt thanks to Bertrand Schmitt, CEO of App Annie and a fellow citizen of the world, who not only offered a reliable source for independent, global app market data, but also had the vision to help bring this book to market. App Annie's insights (and Danielle Levitas, Amir Ghodrati, Lexi Sydow, Jennifer Johnson, Stephanie McArthur) were instrumental in mapping the app revolution out.

Finally, thanks to my husband, my number one fan and the head of my tribe, who brings unconditional support to each of my projects, and to my kids, who finally understand what I do for a living.

ABOUT THE AUTHOR

Aurelie Guerrieri is a leading global catalyst in mobile advertising and a champion for gender diversity. Her specializations are in strategic business development, marketing, international expansion and corporate development.

Aurelie is the Founder & President of Akila One, a growth-focused boutique consultancy working with CEOs of digital, mobile and IoT companies to help them scale their business. Since 2012, Akila One has helped blue chips and rising stars alike leverage mobile for 8-digit revenue expansion and successful exits.

Aurelie began her career with McKinsey & Company covering the telecom and retail sectors. Then, she helped QuinStreet, one of the first digital marketing companies, grow from start-up to publicly-listed company. From there, Aurelie jumped early into the mobile fray with SendMe, which quickly grew to become the leading mobile content provider in the US. Instrumental in the acquisition of the mobile ad network MobPartner by Cheetah Mobile in 2015, she was recruited to launch Cheetah's B2B marketing and business development global operations. Aurelie has also served as President of Women in Wireless, where she has launched 12 international outposts and grown the organization to more than 12,000 members worldwide.

Aurelie is often asked to provide expert commentary in media including Forbes, VentureBeat, Mobile Marketer and The Drum, where she is a regular contributor and creator of the popular Mobile Native column. Sought-after speaker, she has been featured at Mobile Growth Summit, eTail, Casual Connect Asia, the Global Mobile Game Conference, Mobile Apps Unlocked, the Global Mobile Internet Conference, and the Mobile First Summit.

Aurelie holds an MBA and an MSc. In December 2015, she was named one of 25 *Mobile Women to Watch* by Mobile Marketer, considered the most prestigious award for female executives in the mobile marketing industry.

A French native, Aurelie now calls San Francisco home.

CPSIA information can be obtained
at www.ICGtesting.com
Printed in the USA
FSHW021252130819
61006FS

9 780692 892961